AF515517

TARUN TAKSHAY

Build Your Digital Side Hustle (Book 2)

Step-by-Step Guide to Launching & Scaling Online Income Streams

TAKSHAY
DIGITAL ACADEMY

First published by Takshay Digital Academy 2025

Copyright © 2025 by Tarun Takshay

All rights reserved. No part of this publication may be reproduced, stored or transmitted in any form or by any means, electronic, mechanical, photocopying, recording, scanning, or otherwise without written permission from the publisher. It is illegal to copy this book, post it to a website, or distribute it by any other means without permission.

First edition

ISBN: 978-93-5635-778-5

This book was professionally typeset on Reedsy.
Find out more at reedsy.com

To everyone who has ever felt limited by a paycheck, a job title, or fear—this book is for you.

And to my personal inspiration, Lord Krishna, whose wisdom and guidance remind me daily to act with clarity, courage, and purpose.

Contents

Foreword

We are living in a time when opportunities are more abundant than ever before. The digital revolution has made it possible for anyone, anywhere, to start something small — and with the right strategy, scale it into something extraordinary.

From Side Hustle to Financial Freedom is more than a book. It's a movement. It challenges the traditional idea that success only comes from a 9-to-5 job and invites you to explore the exciting world of entrepreneurship, freelancing, and online opportunities.

What makes this book stand out is not just the practical steps it shares, but the mindset it cultivates. It reminds us that financial freedom is not just about money — it's about choices, time, and the ability to design a life you truly love.

If you've ever thought, *"There has to be more than this,"* then you're holding the right book in your hands. Read it carefully, apply its lessons, and watch your side hustle evolve into your gateway to freedom.

Preface

This book was born out of a simple but powerful realization: that true financial freedom doesn't come from working harder, but from working smarter. I wrote *From Side Hustle to Financial Freedom* for every dreamer who has ever felt trapped in the cycle of trading time for money, yet deep down believed that life could be different.

Over the years, I have seen how ordinary people, with limited resources but limitless determination, turned their side hustles into thriving ventures. These are not just stories of money; they are stories of courage, creativity, and resilience.

My goal with this book is not just to share strategies but to guide you through a mindset shift — from employee to entrepreneur, from survival to freedom. If you take these lessons and apply them with consistency, this book can be the bridge between where you are today and where you dream to be.

This is not theory. It's a blueprint. And it works — if you do.

Acknowledgments

No book is ever written alone, and this one is no exception.

First, I want to thank my family, whose unwavering support gave me the strength to pursue my own journey from side hustles to financial independence. Their patience, love, and belief in me have been the bedrock of my efforts.

To my mentors and teachers, who shared their wisdom and experiences so generously, thank you for lighting the path when I needed direction.

I am also deeply grateful to my friends, colleagues, and early readers who offered feedback, encouragement, and honest critique — your voices shaped this book into what it is today.

Lastly, to you, the reader — thank you for picking up this book. Your trust means everything, and my hope is that these pages inspire you to not just dream, but to act.

Prologue

"Dreams don't work unless you do."

Have you ever felt stuck in your 9-to-5, wondering how some people manage to break free and live life on their own terms? That was me not long ago. I knew there had to be a better way—a way to earn more, scale faster, and finally take control of my life.

This book is **for you**: the middle-class worker, the college graduate unsure of your next step, the freelancer dreaming of bigger income, or the housewife who knows she has untapped potential. Together, we'll uncover how small, consistent actions—side hustles, smart money habits, networking, and personal branding—can transform your income and open the doors to **financial freedom**.

I've walked this path myself, and I'll share both my **wins and mistakes**, so you can shortcut your journey. By the end of this book, you'll have a **practical action plan**, real-life strategies, and the confidence to scale your first side hustle into sustainable income.

Are you ready to step out of the middle-class trap and claim the freedom you deserve? Let's get started.

Introduction

We live in an age where the traditional path — study hard, get a stable job, work for decades, and retire — is no longer the guarantee it once was. Costs are rising, job security is shrinking, and the idea of "waiting until retirement to enjoy life" feels outdated. Yet, many people still feel trapped, exchanging their time and energy for a paycheck that barely covers their dreams.

This is where the power of a **side hustle** comes in. What starts as a small, part-time effort can become the spark that transforms your financial life. A side hustle is more than extra income — it's freedom, security, and the possibility of building something truly your own.

In this book, I'll walk you through the mindset, strategies, and practical steps you need to move from simply earning on the side to creating a path toward full financial independence. You'll learn how to identify profitable opportunities, leverage digital platforms, and scale your efforts without burning out.

But most importantly, this book is about **belief**. Believing that you don't have to settle for the limits society places on you. Believing that your skills, passions, and ideas can be turned into income streams. Believing that financial freedom is possible — not just for "other people," but for you.

This is not a quick-fix manual. It's a guide to building long-term freedom, one step at a time. By the end, my hope is that you'll not only have a roadmap, but also the confidence to take action and change your financial future forever.

The journey from side hustle to financial freedom begins now. And it begins with you.

1

Build Your Digital Side Hustle

Finding the right idea is only the beginning.
The real transformation starts when you **build** something from that idea—
when you take action, create value, and put your work into the world.

In Book 1, you discovered how to identify gaps in the market,
find opportunities others don't see,
and choose the right idea for your future.

Now, in Book 2, we move from **clarity to creation**,
from **potential to progress**,
from **idea to income**.
This is where the journey becomes real.

Why the Digital World Is the Best Place to Build a Side Hustle

We are in the greatest era of opportunity in human history.
With nothing more than a laptop and an internet connection,
you can create:

- A digital product

- A service
- A personal brand
- An automated income stream
- A scalable online business

You no longer need:

× Big investment
× A physical store
× Technical skills
× A team
× Years of experience

What you need is the **right strategy**,
the **right execution**,
and the **right mindset**.
That's exactly what this book will give you.

Turning Your Idea Into a Digital Asset

A side hustle becomes powerful the moment it becomes digital.
Why?

Because digital assets allow you to:

✔ Work from anywhere
✔ Earn while you sleep
✔ Reach thousands of people
✔ Scale without extra effort
✔ Build multiple income streams
In the physical world, you are limited.

But in the digital world, your growth becomes **infinite**.

This book will help you transform your idea into a digital structure—

a system that can grow, evolve, and generate income long after you build it.

Execution Is What Separates Dreamers from Achievers

Many people have ideas.
Very few take action.
And even fewer stay consistent long enough to see results.

This book is designed to help you avoid the common traps:
× Overthinking
× Fear of failure
× Waiting for perfect
× Confusion
× Lack of direction

Instead, you will learn:
✔ The exact steps to build your digital side hustle
✔ How to package your idea into a real offer
✔ How to validate your idea before launching
✔ How to set up simple online systems
✔ How to get your first customers
✔ How to grow with confidence

No guesswork.
No overwhelm.
Just clear, practical steps.

From Side Hustle to Stability

A digital side hustle can start small, but with the right structure, it becomes a stable income stream.

This book will show you how to:

- Build a simple online presence
- Create offers people want
- Attract clients or customers
- Use digital tools to save time
- Set up automation that works for you
- Build momentum and consistency
- Turn your hustle into a long-term asset

Your goal is not just to make money. Your goal is to build something that lasts.

You Are No Longer a Beginner

By starting this book, you've already moved beyond the idea stage.
You are stepping into the world of **builders—**
the people who take ideas and transform them into reality.

This is where confidence grows.
This is where action matters.
This is where your millionaire journey becomes visible.
The work you put in now will reward you for years to come.

Let's Build Your Digital Future

Every digital empire begins with a simple build:

- A landing page
- A product
- A service
- A brand
- A system
- A process

And that is exactly what we will create together in this book.

You have the idea.

You have the vision.

Now it's time to build the digital asset that will take you to the next level.

Welcome to **Build Your Digital Side Hustle—**

the actionable guide that turns your clarity into cashflow

and your potential into progress.

Let's begin.

2

Celebrating Your First Wins

"Don't wait for opportunity. Create it." – Anonymous*

Have you ever wondered what it feels like to hold your first ₹10,000 earned entirely on your own? Not from your salary, not from your parents, not from luck—but from your ideas, effort, and persistence? That moment is electrifying.

It's proof that you're capable of more than the 9-to-5 grind, proof that freedom is possible, proof that **your financial destiny is in your hands**.

I remember my first ₹10k vividly. I had been juggling a day job, freelancing late nights, sending countless proposals that went unanswered, and wondering if I was wasting my time. And then… it happened. A client said yes.

The money landed in my account. My heart raced. I felt alive in a way I hadn't before. That wasn't just money—it was **validation**.

It told me: *I can do this. I can create my own income. I can break free from the ordinary.* And that's the first thrill of stepping into your own entrepreneurial journey.

Why Small Wins Are Huge

Most people dismiss small wins because they don't look like "real success." But here's the secret: **big results are built from small, repeated victories**.

After my first ₹10k, I didn't magically know how to make ₹1 lakh. But I knew I could replicate my efforts. I could improve, learn, and scale. That single win **changed my mindset**—from uncertainty to confidence. Every action afterward became easier because I had proof that I *could succeed*.

Mini Story:

My second client came just two weeks later. The difference? Confidence. I wasn't begging for work—I was showing value. That small shift in belief transformed my approach, my negotiations, and ultimately my income.

Identifying Your Wins

Wins aren't always monetary. They can be:

- Sending your first 20 proposals
- Learning a new skill for your side hustle
- Completing a small project
- Getting positive feedback or a referral

Exercise:

List 5 wins from the past 3 months—monetary or non-monetary. Reflect on how each one made you feel and what it taught you.

Celebrating wins, no matter how small, fuels momentum and motivation. Momentum is the hidden currency of success.

Confidence Through Reflection

Confidence isn't inherited; it's earned. I built mine by documenting every win. I'd ask myself:

1. What did I achieve?
2. How did it feel?
3. What can I do next?

These reflections helped me take bolder steps. My first ₹10k led to digital products, more clients, and eventually a small business—all because I acknowledged that **I was capable of growth**.

Mini Story:

After three months of consistent side hustle effort, I launched my first digital course. That first ₹10k win had proven that effort, persistence, and small wins compound into bigger outcomes. I wasn't just trading time for money anymore—I was leveraging skills and systems.

Turning Wins Into Action

A win without action is a memory. I learned to ask:

- What did I learn from this win?
- How can I scale it this month?
- What actionable step can I take this week?

Exercise:

Pick 1 recent win and write down:

- 3 ways to scale it in the next 30 days
- 1 specific action you'll take this week

The Compounding Effect

Consistency is your superpower. Even **1 hour/day** invested in your side hustle may feel small, but over 90 days, it builds skills, revenue, and momentum. Small wins compound like interest, not in your bank account, but in **your confidence, skillset, and income potential**.

Reflection

When I look back at my first ₹10k, it wasn't about money—it was about **belief**. That one win proved that I could challenge the middle-class trap, step out of comfort, and embrace calculated risks. Every win afterward became easier because the first proof existed.

Exercise

1. Reflect on **3 small wins** from the past 30 days.
2. For each win, write:

- What you learned
- How you can scale it this month
- One actionable step for this week

Takeaway

Small wins aren't just celebrations—they're **proof of capability, fuel for momentum, and the foundation of financial freedom**. Celebrate them, learn from them, and use them to scale toward your first big breakthrough.

3

Understanding Market Needs: Finding Your First Opportunity

"Opportunities don't happen. You create them." – Chris Grosser

Have you ever wondered why some people seem to effortlessly find work that pays well, while others struggle to even get a client? The truth is, success in side hustles isn't about luck—it's about understanding **what people truly need and are willing to pay for**.

If you can spot opportunities that others ignore, you can build a business around solving real problems, not chasing random ideas.

When I started my first side hustle, I spent days asking myself: *What does the market want? Where is the gap I can fill?* I had skills in digital marketing, but skills alone weren't enough. I needed demand. That's when I learned the first unspoken rule of side hustles: **the market decides your success, not your passion alone.**

The Middle-Class Mindset vs. Opportunity Mindset

Many middle-class people are trained to play it safe: get a degree, secure a job, follow a predictable path. There's nothing wrong with that—but the problem arises when this mindset becomes a mental trap. Jobs offer security, but they also limit exposure to opportunities.

The difference between someone stuck in the 9-to-5 loop and a successful side hustler is market awareness. You have to stop thinking: "What can I do?" and start thinking: "What does the market need?"

In my first months, I tried to offer generic digital services—social media posts, website graphics—because I liked doing them. The results were discouraging.

Only when I noticed local businesses struggling to generate leads online, and realized I could help them with simple, affordable campaigns, did I get my first paying clients. That insight changed everything. The lesson: the market tells you what's valuable.

How to Spot Opportunities Without Guesswork

Here's the approach I followed—and you can too:

1. **Listen to Complaints:** People constantly complain about problems. Those complaints are goldmines. For example, a friend of mine kept saying that small businesses had no time to manage their Instagram. That's a clear opportunity for social media management services.
2. **Observe Spending Patterns:** Where is money moving? If people are spending on tutoring, online courses, or niche products, there's demand. Your job is to figure out how to solve their pain or offer convenience.
3. **Identify Gaps in Existing Solutions:** Look at products or services in your area. What are they missing? Could you offer faster delivery, better service, or simpler solutions? Even small improvements can generate

revenue quickly.

4. **Test Your Ideas Quickly:** Don't spend months perfecting a product before checking if anyone wants it. I used free social media posts, a basic website, and simple proposals to validate my ideas. Within a week, I knew which services people were willing to pay for.

Exercise:

Take a notebook or digital document and write down **3 recurring problems or complaints** you've noticed in your personal or professional circles. For each problem, jot down **1 possible solution** you could offer.

Finding Your Niche Without Overthinking

Many beginners make the mistake of trying to serve everyone. That's the fastest way to overwhelm yourself and fail. A focused niche allows you to stand out, gain credibility, and deliver value efficiently.

For example, instead of offering "freelance marketing services for anyone," I specialized in **lead generation for local small businesses**. That focus made it easier for me to target clients, charge higher rates, and deliver measurable results.

A friend of mine tried to market to everyone—coaches, restaurants, online sellers, and local shops. He was exhausted and had little success. Once he narrowed to e-commerce stores selling handmade products, he doubled his clients in a month. Focus equals efficiency, clarity, and profitability.

Exercise:

Write down **3 niches or target audiences** where your skills or interests can solve a real problem. Next to each, describe **one problem they face** and **how you could solve it.**

Understanding Willingness to Pay

It's not enough for people to need something—they must be willing to pay for it. Here's a simple test I used in my first hustle:

- Approach 5–10 potential clients and **pitch your solution**.
- Observe reactions: Are they enthusiastic? Do they ask for pricing?
- Only move forward with solutions that people **pay for**, even small amounts.

I initially offered free services to build a portfolio. While I gained experience, I realized free work teaches nothing about **pricing, value, or client expectations**.

When I asked clients to pay even a modest ₹500 for a simple task, suddenly my efforts felt real, clients respected my time, and I understood the value exchange.

Exercise:

Pick **one service or product** idea. Approach 5–10 people in your network and **ask if they'd pay for it**. Record responses. If at least 3–4 say yes, you're onto a viable idea.

Testing Demand Before Diving In

The fastest way to fail is to assume demand without testing. I learned this early: spending months developing services that no one wanted leads to burnout and wasted effort.

Steps to Test Quickly:

- Create a simple landing page or social media post describing your offer.
- Post it in communities where your audience hangs out.
- Collect feedback or small pre-orders.

This approach saved me months of wasted effort and helped me refine offers that **clients actually wanted to pay for**.

Reflection & Mindset Shift

The middle-class mindset teaches you to play safe. The side-hustle mindset teaches you to **listen, observe, and validate**. The key shift is:

- Stop guessing what might sell
- Start observing what people are already paying for
- Test, iterate, and improve

Exercise:

Reflect on the last 30 days:

1. What problems did you notice people complaining about?
2. How could you solve them?
3. Which solution could you test in the next 7–14 days?

Takeaways

- Opportunities are everywhere; you just need to **see them through a market lens**.
- Focus on **real problems people are willing to pay for,** not just what you enjoy.
- **Test ideas quickly** before committing time or money.
- Small, validated wins build confidence and momentum for your next side hustle steps.

Remember: A side hustle without demand is just a hobby. A side hustle with validated demand becomes your first step toward **financial freedom**.

4

Choosing Your First Side Hustle: From Idea to Action

"*The best way to predict the future is to create it." – Peter Drucker*

Have you ever felt stuck, knowing you want more from life, but unsure where to start? The truth is, many middle-class earners dream of financial freedom, but most never take the first step. Choosing your first side hustle can feel overwhelming because there are endless options. The key is **clarity, action, and testing**, not perfection.

When I first started, I spent weeks debating: Should I focus on freelancing? Should I create digital products? Should I try content creation? I wanted something that fit my skills, my schedule, and had paying customers waiting—but I didn't know where to start. The breakthrough came when I realized: **you don't have to be perfect, you just have to start**.

Why Starting Small Matters

Many beginners think they need a perfect, polished idea to succeed. This is the **illusion of perfection** that traps middle-class earners. In reality, starting small lets you **learn, adapt, and grow without risking too much**.

I remember launching my first freelance service with nothing more than a simple Google form to collect orders. It wasn't pretty. It wasn't "perfect." But within the first week, I landed two paying clients. Those small wins fueled my confidence and gave me **proof that I could actually make money outside a 9-to-5 job**.

Starting small also allows you to **test your assumptions**. You might think people want fancy graphics, but maybe they actually just want simple, consistent social media posts. Only by starting small can you discover what truly sells.

Finding Your First Side Hustle

Here's how to identify your first opportunity:

Look at Your Skills and Interests:

Make a list of things you enjoy and skills you already have. Don't limit yourself—include anything from graphic design, writing, tutoring, to hobbies like photography or fitness coaching.

Match Skills to Market Needs:

Refer back to Chapter 2: what problems do people in your potential market have that you could solve? For example, if you're skilled at Excel, you could offer spreadsheet optimization services for small businesses.

Pick Something Actionable:

Avoid ideas that require massive upfront investment or years of learning. Start with what you can offer **this week**, even if it's small.

Validate Your Idea Quickly:

Before spending weeks building your service or product, test it. Talk to 5–10 potential clients, post a social media poll, or offer a beta service at a small fee. The feedback will tell you if you're on the right path.

Exercise:

Write down your **top 5 skills or hobbies**. Next to each, note **one way it could solve someone's problem or provide value**. Circle the one that seems easiest to test this month.

Comparing Popular Side Hustles

Many beginners get paralyzed by choice. Let's break down common options and how they work:

- **Freelancing:** Offers fast cash flow and flexibility. Examples: writing, graphic design, social media management. Pros: Low cost, fast start. Cons: Income tied to hours.
- **Digital Products:** E-books, templates, online courses. Pros: Can generate passive income. Cons: Requires upfront effort and validation.
- **Content Creation:** YouTube, Instagram, blogs, newsletters. Pros: Builds brand authority, audience, and long-term income. Cons: Takes time to monetize.
- **Local Services:** Tutoring, small business support, event planning. Pros: Immediate market, tangible results. Cons: Limited scalability if done solo.

I initially tried freelancing and content creation simultaneously. Freelancing gave quick wins, while content creation slowly built an audience. By combining both, I learned **how to diversify income streams without overcomplicating**.

Exercise:

List 3 side hustle ideas from the above categories that fit your skills and interests. For each, write **one small action you can take this week to test it**.

Overcoming the Fear of Starting

Fear is the number one reason people never launch their first hustle. You may think: *"What if I fail? What if no one pays me?"*

Here's the mindset shift that changed everything for me: **failure is data, not defeat.** Every client rejection, every missed sale, teaches you something. When I started, my first proposal was rejected by three clients. Instead of giving up, I asked why. Their feedback helped me refine my pitch—and my fourth proposal landed ₹5,000 in revenue.

Exercise:

Write down **one fear** holding you back from starting. Next to it, write **one action that challenges that fear** this week. For example: fear of no clients → reach out to 3 potential clients.

Taking the First Step

The most important part of this chapter is action. By the end of this week:

- You should have **chosen your first side hustle**
- Tested it with at least **5 potential clients or users**
- Collected **feedback or first paying orders**

I remember feeling nervous sending my first service offer to a stranger on LinkedIn. I thought I'd be ignored—or worse, laughed at. But the client responded within hours, eager to pay. That first transaction changed my mindset forever: **I was capable, and the market valued my skills**.

Takeaways

- Perfection is the enemy of action. Start small, learn fast.
- Match your skills to market needs; focus on **solving real problems**.
- Validate ideas quickly with real potential clients.
- Fear is natural; action transforms fear into momentum.
- Your first side hustle is proof that you can earn outside a 9-to-5.

Exercise:

Create a simple action plan:

1. Choose your first side hustle.
2. Identify 5 potential clients or users.
3. Send your first offer this week.
4. Collect feedback and adjust your approach.

Remember: The first step is always the hardest. Once you take it, momentum starts to build, small wins compound, and the journey to financial freedom begins

5

Money Mindset & Reinvesting

"Don't let money run your life, let money help you run your life better."
– John Rampton

Have you ever felt like no matter how much you earn, it's never enough? That paycheck disappears faster than you can track it, leaving you wondering why your bank balance never seems to grow. Most middle-class earners think: *"I earn, I save, I spend, repeat."* But here's the truth: **if you want to break free and create wealth, you must change the way you think about money—and how you use it to grow more money.**

When I first started my side hustles, I made a huge mistake: I treated every rupee I earned as instant spending money. I was thrilled with my first ₹5,000, but it vanished within a week. The lesson hit me hard: earning is just the first step; **reinvesting is what multiplies wealth.**

The Middle-Class Money Trap

Most middle-class earners are trapped in a cycle of "income → expense → debt → repeat."

- You work hard to earn more.

- You spend on comfort, gadgets, family expenses.
- You feel financially stuck despite earning more than before.

This happens because our society conditions us to think **money is meant for spending, not multiplying**. Savings alone won't make you rich—investments and reinvestments do.

I remember earning ₹15,000 from my first side hustle month. I was ecstatic. But I spent ₹10,000 immediately on gadgets and dining out. Only ₹5,000 remained, which I reluctantly reinvested in ads and tools. That reinvestment turned into ₹50,000 within two months. That's when I realized: **your money works only when you put it to work**.

Changing Your Money Mindset

A millionaire mindset doesn't mean hoarding cash or taking reckless risks. It's about:

1. **Seeing money as a tool** – to invest in growth, skills, and opportunities.
2. **Prioritizing reinvestment** – every rupee earned should either grow your business, acquire new skills, or expand your network.
3. **Tracking cash flow** – know where every rupee goes; don't let it vanish unnoticed.

Exercise:

Take a look at your last month's spending. Categorize each expense as:

- Essential (bills, groceries)
- Comfort (dining, shopping)
- Investment (courses, tools, ads)

Circle areas where you can **redirect money from comfort to investment**.

Reinvesting Wisely

Not all reinvestments are equal. Here's what worked for me:

1. **Tools & Tech:** Investing in productivity and automation tools early saved hours and multiplied revenue.
2. **Learning & Education:** Every course I bought in the first year returned at least 3x in value, because it helped me improve my side hustle skills.
3. **Marketing & Advertising:** My first ₹5,000 ad spend earned ₹25,000 in revenue—a 5x ROI.

I once hesitated to spend ₹2,000 on a small social media ad campaign. My inner voice said, *"What if I lose it?"* I went ahead anyway. Within days, I landed 3 clients worth ₹12,000 total. That taught me: **risking small amounts on calculated investments is the fastest way to scale income**.

Exercise:

List 3 ways you can reinvest this month's earnings into your side hustle or skills. Next to each, note the expected return or benefit.

Budgeting for Growth

A strong money mindset also means knowing **where to allocate your income**. Here's a simple framework I used:

- **50% Reinvestment:** Tools, marketing, courses, growth opportunities.
- **30% Personal Savings:** Emergency funds, retirement accounts.
- **20% Rewards & Comfort:** Small treats to stay motivated without guilt.

Even if you earn only ₹1,000, this allocation trains your mind to prioritize growth first, comfort second.

Exercise:

Apply the 50-30-20 rule to your next side hustle earnings. Track your progress for 30 days and adjust as needed.

From Small Wins to Compounding Wealth

Money reinvested intelligently grows exponentially. A ₹5,000 investment can become ₹50,000 if done strategically. The key is **patience, consistency, and learning from feedback**.

I started with ₹1,000 investing in ads for a small content service. Month 1: earned ₹2,500. Month 2: reinvested ₹1,500 → earned ₹6,000. Month 3: reinvested ₹3,000 → earned ₹15,000. That simple compounding mindset **turned small wins into financial momentum**, proving that consistent reinvestment beats instant gratification every time.

Takeaways

- Treat money as a tool, not a reward.
- Prioritize reinvestment in skills, tools, and marketing.
- Track every rupee; redirect comfort spending into growth.
- Compounding small wins multiplies wealth faster than waiting for a big paycheck.
- Calculated risks with reinvestment lead to scalable income.

Exercise:

1. Look at your current income streams. How much can you reinvest this month?
2. List 3 reinvestment actions with expected outcomes.
3. Commit to executing **at least one reinvestment action within 7 days**.

Remember: Money doesn't create freedom by sitting idle—it grows when you use it smartly. The mindset of reinvestment separates earners from builders and is the cornerstone of financial independence.

6

Small Wins Build Confidence

"Success is the sum of small efforts repeated day in and day out." – *Robert Collier*

Have you ever felt overwhelmed by the idea of building wealth? The dream of financial freedom can feel so far away, it almost paralyzes you. What if I told you that the key to breaking free isn't a massive leap, but **a series of small, intentional wins that build momentum**?

When I started my first side hustle, I imagined earning ₹50,000 in the first month. Reality hit: my first ₹1,000 felt like a miracle. But that first small win changed everything—it gave me **confidence, clarity, and the courage to scale**.

Why Small Wins Matter

Most beginners think wealth is created overnight—through a viral idea, a lucky investment, or a single big client. The truth is: **confidence compounds.** Each small success builds belief in yourself and your abilities.

Small wins:

1. **Validate your skills:** You see that your effort produces results.

2. **Build momentum:** One small success leads to another.
3. **Reduce fear:** Taking the first step becomes easier after a small victory.
4. **Create a growth mindset:** You start thinking in terms of opportunities instead of limitations.

I remember landing my first ₹2,000 client through freelance writing. It wasn't life-changing financially, but mentally, it was a game-changer. I realized: *"If I can do this, I can do more."* That confidence fueled my next efforts, turning one small project into multiple clients and eventually recurring income.

The Psychology Behind Small Wins

Science backs this up: **dopamine, the "feel-good" hormone, is triggered by accomplishment**—even small ones. Each success reinforces behavior, making you more motivated to take action again.

Most middle-class earners ignore small wins. They wait for perfection or a big break. That's why they stay trapped. The key is **celebrating progress, not perfection.**

How to Identify Small Wins

Small wins aren't random; they're deliberate steps toward a bigger goal. Ask yourself:

- What is the smallest action I can take today that moves me closer to financial growth?
- Can I secure my first client, create my first product, or launch my first ad campaign?
- Which small task will teach me the most and build confidence?

Exercise:

Write down 5 "small wins" you can achieve in the next 7 days. Examples:

1. Send proposals to 3 potential clients.
2. Launch your first social media post promoting your side hustle.
3. Research 1 new tool that can improve productivity.
4. Draft a simple pricing plan for your service.
5. Reinvest ₹500 into ads or a learning resource.

Next to each win, write the **expected outcome and lesson learned.**

Compounding Small Wins

Small wins don't just build confidence—they **compound over time** into meaningful results. Think of them as stepping stones across a river: one step may seem tiny, but cumulatively, they carry you to the other side.

Case Study:

Ravi, a freelancer I mentored, started with a ₹1,000 project. He reinvested half his earnings into learning a new skill. Within 3 months, he had completed 10 small projects, built a portfolio, and secured a ₹15,000 recurring client. None of this would have been possible if he ignored those first small wins.

Exercise:

For each small win you achieve this week, write a one-line reflection:

- What did I learn?
- How does this bring me closer to my financial goal?

Using Small Wins to Scale

Once you start accumulating small wins, the next step is **scaling them systematically**:

1. **Repeat successful actions:** Identify what works and do more of it.

2. **Reinvest earnings:** Use profits from small wins to fund bigger opportunities.
3. **Track results:** Keep a simple journal of actions, outcomes, and lessons.
4. **Celebrate milestones:** Don't wait for the "big win" to feel accomplished.

I once hesitated to pitch for multiple clients, fearing rejection. After landing my first ₹1,000 job, I realized the fear was mostly in my head. I pitched 5 more clients the next day and secured 3. Small wins gave me **momentum and belief in my own abilities**.

Takeaways

- Confidence is built one step at a time—small wins matter.
- Track progress, reflect on lessons, and celebrate achievements.
- Small wins compound into bigger opportunities and income.
- Reinvesting and scaling small wins accelerates growth.
- Fear diminishes as you consistently achieve manageable goals.

Exercise:

1. Choose **one small action per day** that moves your side hustle forward.
2. At the end of the week, list all completed actions and what you learned.
3. Identify **the one action** that created the biggest impact and plan to scale it next week.

Remember: Every millionaire started with small wins. Confidence, momentum, and growth all begin with **the courage to take the first step**. Your first ₹1,000, your first client, your first product—each is a victory worth celebrating.

7

Scaling Your Hustle

"Don't work for money, make money work for you." – Robert Kiyosaki*

Have you ever wondered why some people's side hustles seem to explode while others barely grow? What separates a hobby-level hustle from a scalable income machine? The answer is **intentional scaling**—taking small wins, proven methods, and turning them into reliable, recurring income streams.

When I started my first small online business, I had one client and one product. By month three, I was juggling multiple projects. The secret wasn't working harder—it was **working smarter and building systems to grow sustainably**.

Why Scaling is the Game-Changer

Scaling your hustle isn't just about earning more money. It's about:

1. **Expanding your reach:** More clients, more customers, more visibility.
2. **Optimizing your time:** Systems allow you to earn without doubling your hours.
3. **Reinvesting strategically:** Use profits to fuel growth instead of

spending immediately.

4. **Building credibility:** A side hustle that scales builds a reputation, which opens doors to bigger opportunities.

I remember taking on 10 clients manually at the start—responding to every email and invoice by hand. It was exhausting. Once I invested in automation tools, simple templates, and a structured workflow, I could handle 3x the clients with half the effort. That shift allowed me to reinvest time and energy into acquiring even more business.

Step 1: Identify What's Scalable

Not all tasks are worth scaling. Ask yourself:

- Which of my current activities generate the most income relative to effort?
- What can be standardized, automated, or delegated?
- Which products, services, or offerings have the highest growth potential?

Exercise:

Create a "Hustle Audit" list:

- Write down your current income streams.
- Note how much time each requires.
- Identify one area with high potential for scale.

Step 2: Systematize Your Hustle

Systems are the backbone of growth. Without them, growth is limited by your personal capacity.

Example Strategies:

1. **Templates & Checklists:** Standardize common tasks like proposals,

emails, and delivery processes.

2. **Automation Tools:** Schedule posts, manage clients, and track revenue with simple, free, or low-cost tools.
3. **Delegation:** Outsource repetitive tasks like editing, social media posting, or administrative work.

Case Study:

Ankur, a content creator I follow, started with one YouTube video a week. By systematizing scripts, video editing, and publishing schedules, he scaled to producing 3 videos per week, growing views, subscribers, and revenue.

Exercise:

Pick **one repetitive task** in your side hustle this week. Plan **how you will automate, delegate, or systematize** it. Note potential time saved and impact on growth.

Step 3: Expand Your Offerings

Scaling often means diversifying within your niche. Once your first service or product is stable, consider:

- Upsells: Offer premium versions or additional services.
- Packages: Bundle multiple services together for higher value.
- Complementary Products: Launch products or services that align with your audience's needs.

My first freelance design service earned me ₹5,000/month. When I added a mini-course teaching my design techniques, I earned an additional ₹10,000 without adding extra client work. That small expansion doubled my monthly income.

Exercise:

Brainstorm **3 ways to expand or enhance your existing side hustle offerings**. Note potential earnings and resources needed.

Step 4: Reinvest Profits Strategically

Scaling isn't just about earning more; it's about **reinforcing growth**.

- Allocate a percentage to learning new skills.
- Invest in marketing, tools, or courses that increase efficiency.
- Consider partnerships or collaborations to access larger audiences.

Case Study:

Ravi, my mentee, reinvested ₹5,000 from his first freelancing month into an online course on social media marketing. Within 2 months, he landed 3 new clients who were willing to pay ₹15,000 each. That reinvestment directly multiplied his revenue.

Exercise:

Decide **how much of your first ₹5,000–₹10,000 revenue you will reinvest**. Write down exactly where it will go and why.

Step 5: Track, Analyze, and Improve

Scaling without tracking is guessing. Develop simple metrics:

- How much time per client/project?
- Revenue per task/product?
- Client satisfaction and repeat business?

Reflect monthly: What worked? What didn't? Adjust and optimize constantly.

Exercise:

Create a **Monthly Hustle Tracker**:

- Revenue earned
- Time spent
- Lessons learned
- Next month's focus

Takeaways

- Scaling is intentional; it requires focus on systems, offers, and reinvestment.
- Small wins are the foundation—compound them through smart strategies.
- Automate, delegate, and optimize to multiply your impact without burning out.
- Reinvest profits strategically to fuel sustainable growth.
- Track results to continuously refine your process.

Remember: Scaling doesn't mean doing everything yourself. It's about **working smarter, not harder**, and turning your small wins into a sustainable, growing income stream. Your first ₹10,000 is proof—you can reach ₹50,000, ₹1 lakh, and beyond if you follow these steps consistently.

Next Exercise:

1. List your current side hustle tasks.
2. Identify **one task to systematize or delegate**.
3. Plan **one new offer or upsell** to increase income.
4. Decide **how much revenue to reinvest** this month.
5. Track progress weekly and reflect on lessons.

8

Building Multiple Streams of Hustle Income

"Don't put all your eggs in one basket." – Warren Buffett*

Have you ever wondered why some people seem to make money no matter what happens in the economy, while others struggle to survive? The secret is **multiple income streams**. Imagine your side hustle isn't just one path to money but **several paths that support each other**, creating a safety net and amplifying your earnings.

When I started scaling my first side hustle, I realized that relying solely on freelance clients was risky. Some months I earned ₹20,000, other months barely ₹5,000. That's when I started thinking: "How can I make money even when one income source slows down?" This mindset shift opened doors to multiple revenue streams—and consistent growth.

Why Multiple Streams Matter

Multiple income streams:

1. **Reduce Risk:** If one stream dips, others compensate.

2. **Accelerate Growth:** More streams mean more opportunities for reinvestment.
3. **Build Financial Security:** You're not dependent on one client, job, or platform.
4. **Leverage Skills:** Different streams often use overlapping skills, making growth easier.

When I launched my first freelance design service, I added **a mini-course teaching my techniques** and **affiliate partnerships recommending software I used**. Within months, my revenue wasn't coming from a single client but **3 different sources**, making my hustle more stable and predictable.

Step 1: Identify Potential Income Streams

Think about your current skills and audience. Some common beginner-friendly streams include:

- **Freelancing:** Writing, design, programming, marketing, consulting.
- **Digital Products:** Courses, templates, eBooks, mini-guides.
- **Affiliate Marketing:** Promoting tools, apps, or services you already use.
- **Service Packages:** Bundle consulting, coaching, or freelance work for higher value.
- **Content Monetization:** YouTube, blogging, podcasts, social media sponsorships.

Exercise:

Write down **5 potential income streams** you could realistically start in the next 3 months. Rank them by effort, cost, and potential revenue.

Step 2: Start Small, Stack Strategically

It's tempting to jump into multiple hustles at once, but that's a recipe for burnout. Start with **one primary income stream**, then layer additional streams gradually:

- **Primary Stream:** Your main side hustle that generates revenue first.
- **Secondary Stream:** Related income that leverages the same audience or skills.
- **Tertiary Stream:** Passive or semi-passive income like digital products or affiliate links.

I started with freelancing as my primary stream. Once it was stable, I added a mini-course as a secondary stream. Later, I promoted affiliate tools to my audience as a tertiary stream. Within a year, these three streams together **tripled my income** compared to freelancing alone.

Exercise:

Create a **3-level income stream plan** for your hustle: Primary, Secondary, and Tertiary. Note **how much time, effort, and investment** each requires.

Step 3: Mini Hustle Blueprints

Here are some **practical blueprints** to help you visualize multiple income streams:

Blueprint 1 – Freelance + Course Path

- Primary: Freelance service (₹5k–₹15k/month)
- Secondary: Mini-course teaching your skills (₹2k–₹10k/month)
- Tertiary: Affiliate tools used in your work (₹1k–₹5k/month)

Blueprint 2 – Content + Affiliate Path

- Primary: YouTube channel / Blog monetized via ads
- Secondary: Affiliate marketing for tools or apps
- Tertiary: Digital products or workshops

Blueprint 3 – Service Bundle Path

- Primary: Coaching / Consulting service
- Secondary: Group coaching / membership program
- Tertiary: Templates, checklists, or guides sold online

Exercise:

Pick **one blueprint that fits your skills**. Write down **your first 3 actionable steps** to implement it this month.

Step 4: Reinvest and Multiply

Multiple streams allow you to **reinvest profits strategically**:

- Upgrade tools and automation for efficiency.
- Take short courses to improve your skill set.
- Invest in marketing to reach a broader audience.
- Explore collaborations to create new streams faster.

Case Study:

Rina, a beginner freelancer I mentored, started with content writing. She added a mini-course teaching writing basics, and then affiliate tools she used for productivity. By reinvesting 30% of profits into online ads, she **tripled revenue in 4 months**, without increasing her working hours.

Exercise:

Decide **how much revenue from your first stream you will reinvest** into building the next stream. Document **specific actions and timelines**.

Step 5: Time Management for Multiple Streams

Managing multiple income streams can be overwhelming. Use **time-blocking and batching** to stay focused:

- Allocate specific days for each income stream.
- Batch repetitive tasks to save time.
- Automate wherever possible to prevent burnout.

Exercise:

Create a **weekly time-block schedule** for your income streams. Ensure each stream has **dedicated focus hours** without overlapping.

Takeaways

- Multiple streams reduce risk and accelerate growth.
- Start small: one primary income stream, then layer secondary and tertiary streams.
- Use mini blueprints to structure your hustle growth.
- Reinvest profits strategically to scale faster.
- Manage time carefully to maintain consistency without burnout.

Remember: One stream can feed you; multiple streams can **transform your life**. Each small income adds up, and the combination will give you freedom, security, and exponential growth.

Next Exercise:

1. List 3 income streams you could realistically start this month.
2. Choose a blueprint and write your **first 3 action steps**.
3. Decide **how much revenue to reinvest** in building new streams.

Create a **time-block plan** for managing multiple streams efficiently

9

Building Your Personal Brand

"Your brand is what people say about you when you're not in the room." – Jeff Bezos

Have you ever wondered why some freelancers, creators, or side hustlers seem to attract opportunities effortlessly, while others struggle to get noticed? The difference isn't always skill—it's **brand presence**. Your personal brand is the **magnet that draws clients, collaborations, and opportunities** to you.

When I started scaling my side hustles, I realized that delivering value wasn't enough. People needed to **recognize my expertise, trust me, and remember me**. That's when I focused on building my personal brand. Overnight, networking became easier, clients reached out without me pitching aggressively, and my income streams began to multiply.

Why Personal Branding Matters

1. **Visibility:** People can't hire or follow you if they don't know you exist.
2. **Trust:** A strong personal brand signals credibility and authority.
3. **Leverage:** Opportunities flow in without constant outreach.
4. **Scalability:** Your brand amplifies all your income streams.

I once worked silently on a freelance project for months. When I started sharing my process, tips, and results on social media, inquiries flooded in. Just by **showing my journey**, I became more visible than competitors with the same skill set. This taught me that **brand perception often matters more than raw talent**.

Step 1: Define Your Brand Identity

Your brand is not just a logo or a website—it's a **clear message about who you are, what you offer, and why people should care**.

Ask yourself:

- What is my unique skill or expertise?
- Who is my target audience?
- What problem do I solve for them?
- What values do I want to communicate?

Exercise:

Write a **2–3 sentence brand statement** answering the above questions. This is your personal brand elevator pitch.

Step 2: Show Up Consistently

Consistency is the heartbeat of branding. You don't need fancy designs or viral content—just **regular, value-driven presence**.

- Share your journey, tips, and lessons learned.
- Post 2–3 times per week on a chosen platform (LinkedIn, Instagram, YouTube, or blog).
- Engage with your audience through comments, DMs, and collaborations.

I started posting short tutorials and insights on Instagram every week. Within 3 months, I gained a small but highly engaged following. Those followers turned into clients, course students, and collaborators. **Consistency created credibility** and multiplied opportunities.

Exercise:

Create a 7-**day content plan**: what you will post each day, including tips, lessons, or personal stories.

Step 3: Leverage Multiple Channels

You don't have to be everywhere, but using **multiple channels strategically** expands reach:

- **Social Media:** Share insights, behind-the-scenes, client success stories.
- **Blog or Medium:** Long-form content builds authority and helps with discovery.
- **Email Newsletter:** Build a direct line to your audience and sell services/products.
- **YouTube / Podcasts:** Showcase expertise, personality, and stories.

Exercise:

Select 2 **platforms to start with**, and create your **first piece of branded content** for each.

Step 4: Authentic Storytelling

People connect with **stories, not sales pitches**. Share your journey, failures, small wins, and lessons learned. This makes your brand human and relatable.

I once shared my first failed freelance attempt—losing ₹5,000 due to inexperience. That post got more engagement than any technical tip I had shared. People related to my struggle, trusted my guidance, and later became clients.

Exercise:

Write a **short story (200–300 words)** about a challenge you overcame in your side hustle or career. Share it online this week.

Step 5: Build Authority Through Value

A strong personal brand isn't about bragging—it's about **helping others achieve results**.

- Share tips, hacks, and tutorials.
- Highlight results you helped clients or peers achieve.
- Use testimonials and case studies to reinforce credibility.

Exercise:

List **3 ways you can provide tangible value** to your audience this month. Create one piece of content for each.

Step 6: Monetize Your Brand

Once you've established visibility and trust, your personal brand can **amplify your income streams**:

- Freelance clients will find you.
- Courses, workshops, or coaching can sell faster.
- Affiliate or product promotions become more effective.

Case Study:

Rahul, a beginner content creator I mentored, started with YouTube tutorials. Within 6 months, his small following became a **paid course audience**, and he monetized affiliate tools. His personal brand **turned his side hustle into his main income source**.

Exercise:

Identify **one monetization path** tied to your brand this month (course, service, affiliate, etc.) and draft a **launch plan with 3 actionable steps**.

Key Takeaways

- Your personal brand is your **magnet for opportunities**.
- Define your identity, be consistent, and share your authentic story.
- Use 2–3 strategic channels to amplify reach.
- Provide value first; monetize second.
- A strong brand multiplies all your side hustle income streams.

Remember: People don't just buy services—they buy **trust, results, and the story behind the person delivering them**. Your brand is that story.

Next Exercise:

1. Write your **brand statement** in 2–3 sentences.
2. Plan your **first** 7 **days of content** and post it.
3. Choose **2 platforms** to start building presence.
4. Share your **authentic story** online.
5. Identify **one monetization path** tied to your brand and draft actionable steps.

10

Networking & Collaboration

"Your network is your net worth." – Porter Gale

Have you ever felt like you're working hard on your side hustle but progress feels slow, and opportunities aren't coming? What if I told you that the fastest way to accelerate growth isn't just working harder—but **connecting with the right people**?

When I started my first side hustles, I thought I could do everything alone. I spent weeks perfecting a service offer, only to realize that **one strategic connection could have saved me months of trial and error**. That moment changed my perspective: success grows faster when you **collaborate, not just compete**.

Why Networking & Collaboration Matter

1. **Accelerates Learning:** Mentors and peers teach lessons you'd spend years figuring out alone.
2. **Opportunities Multiply:** Collaborators bring clients, partnerships, and joint ventures.
3. **Credibility Boost:** Being associated with experienced people builds trust with your audience.

4. **Idea Exchange:** Networking sparks ideas that grow your income streams faster.

I remember reaching out to a fellow freelancer who had built a six-figure consulting business. A single coffee chat gave me **insights that doubled my side hustle revenue within three months**. That one connection also led to collaborative projects that exposed me to new audiences.

Step 1: Identify Your Network

Your network isn't just high-profile mentors—it includes:

- **Peers:** People at the same hustle level for brainstorming and accountability.
- **Mentors:** Experienced individuals who guide and correct your mistakes.
- **Potential Clients:** Those who can pay for your services or products.
- **Collaborators:** People whose skills complement yours for joint projects.

Exercise:

List **10 people** in these categories you want to connect with this month. Include one actionable step for each (DM, email, LinkedIn message, or coffee chat).

Step 2: Build Genuine Relationships

Networking isn't about asking for favors—it's about **giving first**.

- Help peers solve problems.
- Share resources, tips, or contacts freely.
- Engage consistently through messages, social media comments, or collaboration offers.

I once helped a fellow side hustler optimize their website for free. A month later, they referred three clients to me. I realized that **giving before asking creates trust and multiplies opportunities**.

Exercise:

Identify **one person you can help this week** without expecting anything in return.

Step 3: Attend Events & Online Communities

Even if you're busy, you can expand your network without traveling:

- **Local workshops or meetups:** Meet peers and mentors in person.
- **Online communities:** Facebook groups, LinkedIn forums, Reddit subreddits, Discord channels.
- **Webinars & virtual events:** Learn and connect with experts worldwide.

Exercise:

Join **2 relevant online communities** this week and introduce yourself in a meaningful, value-added way.

Step 4: Collaboration for Growth

Collaboration can multiply your results faster than solo work:

- **Joint Projects:** Partner with someone who has complementary skills.
- **Guest Content / Podcast:** Share each other's audience to expand reach.
- **Mentorship / Accountability Partnerships:** Accelerate learning and consistency.

Case Study:

Ankur, a friend I met through a freelancer community, and I decided to co-create a digital course. Each of our audiences brought in **over ₹50,000 in combined sales within the first month**. This partnership accelerated our growth far faster than individual efforts.

Exercise:
Identify **one potential collaborator** and draft a **3-step plan to propose a small project or partnership** this month.

Step 5: Maintain & Nurture Relationships

Networking is not one-time; it's a long-term effort:

- Schedule check-ins with key contacts.
- Celebrate their wins publicly.
- Share resources, insights, or introductions regularly.

I still keep in touch with my first mentor from six years ago. Occasionally, I send him insights, celebrate his milestones, or ask for advice. That long-term relationship has brought **consistent referrals and business growth** over the years.

Exercise:
Pick **3 existing contacts** and send meaningful messages to **reconnect and add value** this week.

Key Takeaways

- Networking is **multiplicative**: one connection can open multiple doors.
- Give first, build trust, and provide value before asking for anything.
- Attend events, join communities, and proactively seek collaboration.
- Long-term relationships create **sustained business growth**.

Remember: Success rarely happens in isolation. The people you surround yourself with determine **how fast and far your side hustles can grow**. Your network is the ladder that lifts your hustle beyond limits.

Next Exercises:

1. List 10 people in your network categories (peers, mentors, clients, collaborators).
2. Take one step this week to **help someone** in your network.
3. Join 2 online communities and introduce yourself meaningfully.
4. Identify one collaboration opportunity and draft a proposal.

Reconnect with 3 existing contacts to add value

11

Mastering Multiple Side Hustles

"Don't put all your eggs in one basket—but know how to manage them all at once." – Unknown*

Have you ever wondered how some people seem to effortlessly earn from multiple sources, while others struggle to grow just one? Could you be missing out on a bigger financial picture simply because you're focusing on a single hustle?

When I started my journey, I had only one freelance project. I worked late nights, weekends, and was proud to earn my first ₹10k. But I realized quickly that **one hustle can only take you so far**. Scaling required **multiple income streams, smart time management, and leveraging my growing network**.

Why Multiple Side Hustles Matter

1. **Income Diversification:** If one source slows, others keep cash flowing.
2. **Skill Expansion:** Each hustle teaches you new skills that benefit all others.
3. **Opportunity for Passive Income:** Some hustles can eventually run with minimal attention.
4. **Faster Financial Independence:** Multiple streams accelerate wealth-

building and reduce reliance on any single job.

After my first freelance gig stabilized, I started a small digital product alongside it. Then I explored affiliate income from tools I used daily. Within a year, **my income had multiplied 4x**, and I was finally feeling in control of my financial future.

Step 1: Evaluate Your Hustles

Not every hustle is worth scaling. Ask yourself:

- Does it have growth potential?
- Can I systematize or outsource parts of it?
- Will it complement my other hustles or compete for my time?

Exercise:
List **all current income sources** and rate them on potential growth, effort required, and synergy with other hustles. Decide which to **scale, maintain, or pause**.

Step 2: Prioritize & Schedule

Balancing multiple hustles is about **time allocation and focus**.

- Create a weekly schedule for each hustle.
- Dedicate prime hours to the hustle with highest ROI.
- Batch similar tasks across projects for efficiency.

Mini-Blueprint:

- Hustle A (highest revenue potential) → Morning focus 3x/week
- Hustle B (mid-term growth) → Evening 2x/week
- Hustle C (passive/affiliate) → Automate & check weekly

Exercise:

Draft a 7-**day time-block plan** for all your hustles. Include 1 hour daily for learning and networking.

Step 3: Leverage Your Network

Connections are multiplier forces for multiple hustles:

- Collaborators can help you manage tasks across hustles.
- Mentors can guide you to prioritize high-impact hustles.
- Peers can provide leads, referrals, and skill-sharing.

I once connected with a content creator through a networking event. They helped me market one of my digital products to a new audience. Simultaneously, I referred freelance clients to them. **Both of our hustles benefited, creating a win-win synergy**.

Exercise:

Identify **2 contacts from your network** who could help you scale or cross-promote any of your hustles. Reach out this week.

Step 4: Systems & Automation

The key to managing multiple hustles is **automation**:

- Use scheduling tools for social media and content.
- Automate invoicing and payments.
- Set reminders for follow-ups and deadlines.

When I started automating my affiliate promotions and client follow-ups, I could focus more on growth strategies instead of repetitive tasks. This gave me **hours every week** to either start new hustles or scale existing ones.

Exercise:

List **3 processes in your hustles that can be automated or delegated**. Take one step this week to implement it.

Step 5: Measure, Reflect & Adjust

Scaling multiple hustles requires regular assessment:

- Track revenue, time spent, and growth for each hustle.
- Adjust focus if a project underperforms.
- Celebrate small wins to maintain motivation.

Mini-Checklist:

- Weekly review: Revenue, clients, progress
- Monthly reflection: ROI, synergy with other hustles
- Quarterly adjustment: Scale, pause, or pivot hustles

Exercise:

Set up a **simple tracking sheet or journal**. Review your hustles weekly and note what's working, what isn't, and what to improve.

Takeaways

- Multiple side hustles multiply your **learning, income, and opportunities**.
- Time management, prioritization, and automation are essential.
- Your network can accelerate growth and open doors you can't reach alone.
- Consistent tracking ensures you're scaling efficiently without burning out.

Remember: You don't need to do everything perfectly. You need to **do**

multiple things consistently, learn fast, and optimize smarter. Your side hustles are the foundation for financial freedom—and the more strategically you stack them, the faster you climb.

Next Exercises:

1. List all your current and potential hustles with growth potential.
2. Time-block each hustle in a weekly plan.
3. Identify 2 network contacts to collaborate or cross-promote.
4. Automate or delegate at least 1 repetitive task this week.
5. Set up a weekly review system to measure progress and adjust.

12

Building Your Personal Brand

"Your brand is what people say about you when you're not in the room." – Jeff Bezos

Have you ever wondered why some side hustlers effortlessly attract clients, followers, and opportunities while others struggle despite working just as hard? Could the difference be **how they are perceived** in their industry?

When I started freelancing, I delivered quality work, but I struggled to get repeat clients. It wasn't about skill—it was about **visibility, trust, and positioning**. Once I focused on building my personal brand, things changed: clients reached out, collaborations appeared, and my hustles started scaling faster than I had imagined.

Why Personal Branding Matters

1. **Trust & Credibility:** People buy from those they know, like, and trust.
2. **Attracting Clients & Opportunities:** A strong brand brings inbound inquiries.
3. **Higher Value & Pricing Power:** Branding allows you to charge more confidently.

4. **Foundation for Multiple Hustles:** One strong brand can support freelancing, products, and content simultaneously.

I remember posting my first series of tutorials online. At first, barely anyone noticed. But after consistently sharing insights and client successes, I started receiving messages like: *"I want to work with you"* and *"Can you guide me on starting my own hustle?"* My personal brand became a **magnet for opportunities**.

Step 1: Define Your Brand Identity

Ask yourself:

- What am I passionate about?
- What problems do I solve?
- Who is my ideal audience?

Your brand identity is **not just a logo or color palette**—it's **your story, expertise, and personality expressed consistently**.

Exercise:

Write a **50-word personal brand statement** that answers: "I help [audience] achieve [result] by [your method]." Example: *"I help freelancers build their first ₹10k/month side hustle by teaching them simple, actionable strategies they can implement today."*

Step 2: Position Yourself as an Expert

- Share results, case studies, and learnings from your hustles.
- Write blogs, create videos, or post social media updates.
- Be generous with value, not just promotion.

When I began sharing client success stories and small wins from my hustles, I started receiving **referrals organically**. People trusted my methods because I demonstrated results.

Exercise:
Post **one valuable tip or case study this week** on your preferred platform. Track engagement and learn what resonates.

Step 3: Build Consistent Visibility

- Post regularly to stay top-of-mind.
- Engage with your audience: answer questions, comment, and share insights.
- Maintain consistency in your messaging and visual identity.

Mini-Blueprint:

- Platform focus: LinkedIn, Instagram, or YouTube (choose 1–2)
- Posting cadence: 2–3 posts per week
- Engagement: reply to every comment or message within 24 hours

Exercise:
Create a **1-week content plan**: 3 posts, 2 stories, 1 live session or video. Stick to it.

Step 4: Leverage Testimonials & Social Proof

- Showcase client success stories.
- Highlight milestones: revenue growth, completed projects, or collaborations.
- Encourage reviews and recommendations.

I once featured a freelancer I mentored who hit their first ₹50k month. Sharing this success not only inspired others but also **built my credibility**

as a trusted guide, leading to more high-value clients.

Exercise:

Ask **3 satisfied clients or collaborators** for a testimonial this week. Use it in your online profiles or portfolio.

Step 5: Extend Your Brand Across Multiple Hustles

Your personal brand should **support all your side hustles**:

- Freelancing → showcase your expertise
- Digital products → demonstrate authority
- Content → engage and educate your audience

Exercise:

List **all your current and potential hustles**. Write 1–2 sentences for each, explaining **how your brand positions you as the go-to person**.

Key Takeaways

- A strong personal brand **builds trust, attracts clients, and accelerates growth**.
- Position yourself consistently, share results, and engage with your audience.
- Testimonials and social proof multiply credibility.
- One personal brand can amplify multiple side hustles simultaneously.

Remember: People don't just buy products or services—they **buy confidence, trust, and expertise**. Your brand is the bridge that turns your side hustles into sustainable financial freedom.

Next Exercises:

1. Draft your **50-word personal brand statement**.
2. Share **one valuable tip or case study** this week online.
3. Build a **1-week content plan** for posting and engagement.
4. Collect **3 testimonials** from clients or collaborators.
5. Map **how your brand supports all your hustles** in 1–2 sentences each.

13

Networking & Collaboration

"Your network is your net worth." – Porter Gale

Have you ever wondered why some side hustlers skyrocket while others stay stuck, even if they have similar skills? Could it be that **who you know** matters just as much as **what you know**?

Early in my journey, I tried to do everything alone—freelancing, content creation, small digital products. I worked hard but felt stuck. Then I realized: **building the right connections could accelerate my growth exponentially.**

Once I started networking strategically, doors opened that I didn't even know existed—collaborations, referrals, and mentorship that helped me multiply my income.

Why Networking & Collaboration Matter

1. **Access to Opportunities:** The right contacts can lead to clients, partnerships, and new ventures.
2. **Knowledge & Mentorship:** Learning from experienced people reduces trial-and-error.

3. **Collaboration for Growth:** Joint projects or co-branded offerings expand reach.
4. **Accountability & Motivation:** Connecting with like-minded hustlers keeps you consistent and inspired.

I remember reaching out to a mid-level freelancer in my niche. Initially, it was just to exchange ideas, but that connection turned into a joint project that generated **₹50,000 in revenue in one month**—all because we combined our skills and audience.

Step 1: Identify Your Network Targets

Think about these groups:

- **Peers:** People hustling in similar fields.
- **Mentors:** Those ahead of you who can provide guidance.
- **Collaborators:** Individuals whose skills complement yours.
- **Potential Clients:** Decision-makers who need your services.

Exercise:

Write a list of **10 people** you want to connect with this month across these four groups. Include one sentence on **why connecting with each would be mutually beneficial**.

Step 2: Start with Value

Networking isn't about asking for favors—it's about giving first.

- Share insights, tips, or resources.
- Celebrate their wins publicly.
- Offer to collaborate or contribute without expecting immediate return.

I reached out to a content creator whose audience overlapped with mine. I offered a free mini-guide for their newsletter. That simple act of value led to a **joint webinar**, generating both exposure and revenue.

Exercise:

Identify **one person this week** to provide value to, whether through advice, content, or collaboration.

Step 3: Leverage Online Platforms

- **LinkedIn:** Build credibility and connect with professionals.
- **Instagram / YouTube:** Engage with creators and potential clients.
- **Freelance Communities:** Join forums, Slack groups, or Discord channels.

Mini-Blueprint:

- Spend 15–30 minutes daily commenting, sharing insights, or messaging peers.
- Participate in 1–2 online events or webinars per month.
- Keep track of connections and follow up consistently.

Exercise:

Create a **weekly networking schedule**: list the platforms, daily engagement actions, and follow-up reminders.

Step 4: Collaborate Strategically

Look for **win-win opportunities**:

- Co-create products or services.
- Host webinars or workshops together.
- Share each other's audience through content or promotions.

A collaboration with a freelancer complementing my skills brought in **3 new high-value clients** in one month. We split responsibilities, leveraged our audiences, and both earned more than we would have alone.

Exercise:

Draft a **Collaboration Plan**: list 3 potential partners, the type of collaboration, and one action step to approach them this week.

Step 5: Maintain & Nurture Relationships

- Follow up regularly.
- Celebrate their wins.
- Offer help whenever possible.

Tip: Treat relationships like a **garden**. Regular care produces long-term growth.

Exercise:

Pick **5 key connections** and write personalized messages this week—check-in, share an update, or offer value.

Key Takeaways

- Your network directly impacts your opportunities, growth, and revenue potential.
- Always lead with value before expecting anything in return.
- Collaborations amplify reach, trust, and credibility.
- Consistent follow-up and nurturing turn casual connections into long-term partnerships.

Remember: **Alone you can go fast, but together you can go far.** Building meaningful relationships is not optional—it's essential for multiplying your side hustle earnings and achieving financial freedom.

Next Exercises:

1. Make a **list of 10 people** you want to connect with this month.
2. Identify **one way to add value** to a connection this week.
3. Build a **weekly networking schedule** for engagement and follow-up.
4. Draft a **Collaboration Plan** with 3 potential partners.
5. Write personalized messages to **5 key connections** to nurture relationships.

This chapter naturally sets up **Chapter 13 – Mastering Multiple Side Hustles**, where readers will learn how to juggle and scale multiple income streams while leveraging the networks they've built.

14

Mastering Multiple Side Hustles

"D*on't put all your eggs in one basket—but make sure each basket grows your wealth." –*

Have you ever felt like one income stream just isn't enough? Maybe your first side hustle brought in ₹10k, but you worry: what if it stops tomorrow? What if the client disappears, or the market changes?

That's exactly what I felt early in my journey. I had a single freelancing gig, and while it gave me hope, it wasn't enough. I realized **to truly escape the middle-class trap, I needed multiple, complementary income streams**.

That's when I began experimenting—freelancing, creating small digital products, and even affiliate partnerships. The learning curve was steep, but the growth and financial security were undeniable.

Why Multiple Hustles Matter

1. **Risk Mitigation:** If one income stream slows down, others keep flowing.
2. **Skill Diversification:** Different hustles teach different skills—marketing, sales, product creation.

3. **Accelerated Growth:** Combining revenue streams multiplies your total earnings faster.
4. **Financial Freedom:** More income streams = faster reinvestment → faster scaling.

I started with a freelance copywriting gig. Within three months, I added a small online course based on my expertise. Then I joined an affiliate program in the same niche. Within six months, my total income was **triple what I earned from freelancing alone**, and I wasn't stressed about a single client leaving.

Step 1: Identify Complementary Side Hustles

Look for hustles that:

- **Use overlapping skills** (example: writing → copywriting, content creation, course).
- **Target similar audiences** (example: freelancers → offer coaching or templates).
- **Require manageable time investment** (so you don't burn out).

Exercise:

List **3 hustles** you could start this month. For each, write one line on how it complements your existing hustle.

Step 2: Time Allocation & Prioritization

Juggling multiple hustles requires **strategic time-blocking**.

- **Primary Hustle:** 50–60% focus—your main revenue driver.
- **Secondary Hustle:** 20–30%—complementary income.
- **Tertiary Hustle:** 10–20%—testing new opportunities.

Personal Tip:

I blocked **1 hour per day** for my secondary hustle and **2 hours on weekends** for my tertiary experiments. Within two months, the tertiary hustle became a secondary income stream.

Exercise:

Create a **weekly schedule** allocating hours for each hustle. Include specific tasks for each block.

Step 3: Reinvest Wisely

Every additional hustle generates money—don't spend it all immediately.

- Reinvest in **skills** (courses, tools).
- Reinvest in **marketing** (ads, promotions).
- Reinvest in **automation tools** to save time.

After earning ₹15k from my first two side hustles, I invested ₹5k into an email automation tool. Within a month, it generated ₹20k in recurring sales—more than doubling my investment.

Exercise:

Identify **one expense this month** that will help scale any of your hustles.

Step 4: Systems & Automation

Multiple income streams can get messy without systems.

- **Task Lists & Calendar:** Track deadlines and commitments.
- **Automation Tools:** Email sequences, payment collection, social posting.
- **Templates:** Standardize repetitive tasks for faster execution.

Exercise:

Create a **system checklist** for each hustle: list the tasks, tools, and recurring processes.

Step 5: Collaboration & Outsourcing

Leverage other people's skills to scale faster:

- **Freelancers:** Delegate tasks that drain your energy.
- **Partners:** Co-create content, products, or marketing campaigns.
- **Mentors:** Seek advice on scaling strategies.

I hired a virtual assistant to handle client onboarding for one hustle. This freed 10 hours a week, which I used to develop a second digital product. Within three months, revenue from both streams **doubled**.

Exercise:
List **one task per hustle** you could delegate this month and identify potential collaborators.

Key Takeaways

- Multiple side hustles reduce risk and accelerate income growth.
- Focus on complementary hustles that align with your skills and audience.
- Reinvest profits strategically to scale faster.
- Systems, automation, and delegation are essential for managing multiple streams.

Remember: **Your first hustle is just the beginning. Each additional stream multiplies your earning potential and brings you closer to true financial freedom.**

Next Exercises:

1. Identify **3 complementary hustles** you can start.
2. Create a **weekly time-block schedule** for all hustles.
3. Plan one **reinvestment** for scaling.
4. Build a **system checklist** for each hustle.
5. List **tasks to delegate or collaborate** this month.

15

Building Your Personal Brand

"Your brand is what people say about you when you're not in the room." – Jeff Bezos

Have you ever wondered why some freelancers, side hustlers, or entrepreneurs seem to attract clients effortlessly while others struggle? The answer is simple: **they have a personal brand that commands attention and trust.**

When I first started my side hustles, I treated every project as just a transaction. I thought, "If I deliver good work, people will come." But I learned quickly—without a **brand**, I was invisible in a sea of competitors.

That's when I shifted my focus: I started sharing my journey, my insights, and my expertise publicly. Within months, people began reaching out to me, clients trusted me faster, and opportunities multiplied.

Why Personal Branding Matters

1. **Credibility & Trust:** A clear brand makes people confident in working with you.
2. **Visibility & Recognition:** When your audience knows your name,

skills, and values, you stand out.

3. **Premium Pricing:** People pay more for someone they perceive as an expert.
4. **Opportunities Multiply:** Partnerships, collaborations, speaking gigs, and higher-paying clients come naturally.

I once had a small digital product that barely sold. After I shared a story on LinkedIn about my struggles and solutions, it sold out in 24 hours. My personal brand—my story—became the magnet for sales.

Step 1: Define Your Unique Value

Ask yourself:

- What am I known for?
- What problem do I solve better than anyone else?
- What values do I want my audience to associate with me?

Exercise:

Write a **personal brand statement** in one sentence. Example:

"I help freelancers build recurring income streams by teaching practical, actionable strategies they can implement today."

Step 2: Choose Your Platforms

You don't need to be everywhere—focus on where your audience spends time.

- **LinkedIn:** Ideal for freelancers and B2B services.
- **Instagram / YouTube:** Great for storytelling, content creation, and digital products.
- **Blogs / Medium:** Position yourself as a thought leader.
- **Email Newsletter:** Direct connection with your audience.

Personal Tip:

I started with LinkedIn and email because my target clients were professionals and small business owners. Consistency was key—posting 3–4 times per week and sharing actionable insights built trust fast.

Exercise:

Select **2–3 platforms** to focus on. Commit to posting at least **once per week** for the next month.

Step 3: Share Your Story

People connect with stories, not sales pitches.

- Share **journeys**, including struggles and lessons learned.
- Share **wins**, even small ones—they inspire others.
- Share **insights**, tips, and actionable advice.

I once shared a post about my first ₹1,000 side hustle milestone and the mistakes I made. The engagement was massive, and several readers became clients because they trusted me from my story.

Exercise:

Write **one story post** that shares a personal lesson or success from your side hustle.

Step 4: Position Yourself as an Expert

- Teach, don't sell—educate your audience.
- Offer free tips, templates, or insights to build credibility.
- Share results from your work to demonstrate authority.

Personal Tip:

I created a small "Side Hustle Starter Kit" PDF. I gave it away for free, and it established my authority. People trusted me enough to buy my first paid course shortly after.

Exercise:

Create **one piece of free value** (PDF, checklist, video) you can share with your audience this month.

Step 5: Consistency is Key

A personal brand is like a plant—it grows slowly and needs daily attention.

- Post regularly.
- Engage with comments and messages.
- Maintain your brand voice and values consistently.

Consistency made all the difference. I posted for six months almost daily before seeing tangible results. By month seven, leads were coming without me chasing clients.

Exercise:

Set a **3-month posting schedule** for your chosen platforms. Include content ideas, post type, and frequency.

Key Takeaways

- Your personal brand is your silent salesperson.
- Storytelling builds connection, credibility, and trust.
- Focus on platforms that reach your target audience.
- Consistency, free value, and expertise amplify your reach.

Remember: **Your personal brand is not just your logo or color scheme—it's the reputation, trust, and value you consistently provide.**

Next Exercises:

1. Define your **personal brand statement**.
2. Choose **2–3 platforms** to focus on.
3. Share **one personal story post** this week.
4. Create **one free value asset** to build authority.
5. Plan a **3-month content schedule** for consistency.

16

Scaling Your Network & Collaborations

"Your network is your net worth." – Porter Gale

Have you ever wondered why some people seem to attract opportunities effortlessly, while others work hard yet stay stuck? The secret often isn't just skill—it's **who you know and how you connect.**

When I first started my side hustles, I focused solely on delivering work. I ignored building relationships, thinking results alone would speak for themselves. Big mistake. I learned that even a brilliant skill can remain unnoticed without a **network of the right people**.

Why Networking Matters

1. **Opportunities Multiply:** Collaborations, partnerships, and referrals come from the people you know.
2. **Learning & Growth:** Surrounding yourself with like-minded individuals accelerates your skills and insights.
3. **Trust & Credibility:** When respected peers endorse you, your credibility skyrockets.
4. **Scale Faster:** With the right collaborations, you can achieve results that would take years alone.

I met a fellow freelancer at a local meet-up. We started collaborating on small projects. Within six months, our combined efforts landed us clients that individually we could never have reached. That collaboration became a consistent income stream and even led to a joint course launch.

Step 1: Identify Your Network Targets

Ask yourself:

- Who can teach me new skills?
- Who can refer clients or opportunities?
- Who could I collaborate with for mutual growth?

Exercise:
Create a **list of 10 people** you admire or could learn from. Include peers, potential mentors, and collaborators. Note down how you could approach them this month.

Step 2: Give Before You Receive

Networking is not about asking for favors immediately—it's about **providing value first**.

- Share knowledge freely.
- Promote other people's work.
- Offer help without expecting instant return.

Personal Tip:
I helped a colleague with free social media guidance. Six months later, they referred me to their client, which became my first ₹50,000 side project. Giving first builds goodwill and long-term partnerships.

Exercise:

Identify **one person in your list** and offer help, advice, or a collaboration this week.

Step 3: Build Meaningful Collaborations

Collaboration amplifies results:

- **Joint Projects:** Combine expertise for higher value offerings.
- **Cross-Promotion:** Share each other's content or products to reach new audiences.
- **Learning Partnerships:** Partner with someone to skill-up faster.

I partnered with a content creator to bundle our services. Our combined offer was more attractive, and we landed a client willing to pay **double** what I usually charged. Collaboration multiplied revenue without doubling work.

Exercise:
Draft **one potential collaboration plan** with a peer or expert in your field. Include steps, roles, and timeline.

Step 4: Attend Events & Online Communities

Your environment shapes your network:

- **Local meet-ups & workshops:** Ideal for making in-person connections.
- **Online forums & LinkedIn groups:** Expand reach and engage with experts.
- **Masterminds / Peer groups:** Surround yourself with ambitious peers.

Personal Tip:
Joining a small online mastermind group changed everything for me. The ideas, accountability, and connections accelerated my side hustle growth far faster than working alone.

Exercise:

Join **one relevant online group** or attend a local event this month. Set a goal to **connect with 3 new people** at each event.

Step 5: Keep Nurturing Relationships

Networking isn't a one-time effort—it's an ongoing process.

- Follow up with your contacts regularly.
- Share your wins and insights.
- Celebrate others' achievements.

I maintain a simple monthly email to my key contacts sharing updates, lessons, or helpful tips. It keeps me top-of-mind, and several opportunities came from people remembering me because of this small habit.

Exercise:

Create a **relationship map** of your contacts and schedule **monthly touchpoints** to nurture them.

Key Takeaways

- Your network can accelerate opportunities, learning, and revenue.
- Give before expecting return; provide value first.
- Collaborate strategically to multiply results.
- Attend events, join communities, and nurture relationships consistently.

Remember: **It's not about collecting contacts—it's about cultivating meaningful relationships that lead to growth, opportunities, and financial freedom.**

Next Exercises:

1. List 10 potential mentors, peers, or collaborators.
2. Offer help to at least 1 person on your list.
3. Draft a collaboration plan with a peer.
4. Join 1 online community or attend 1 event.
5. Create a monthly relationship nurturing schedule.

17

Monetizing Your Brand & Network

"Your brand is your promise; your network is your leverage."

Have you ever wondered why some people effortlessly convert attention into income while others struggle to monetize even a loyal following? The secret lies in **knowing your value, leveraging relationships, and creating offers people can't resist.**

I learned this the hard way. When I first started sharing my knowledge online, I had a growing audience, friends in the industry, and even some repeat clients—but I struggled to turn these connections into consistent revenue.

Everything changed when I realized **monetization isn't about selling—it's about structuring offers, building trust, and providing real value.**

Step 1: Define Your Value Proposition

Before monetizing your network, you need clarity on **what you offer**:

- What problems can you solve for your audience?
- What unique skills or experiences set you apart?

- How can your network benefit from collaborating with you?

I had skills in digital marketing and a growing network of freelancers. Instead of pitching random services, I packaged my expertise into a **consultation + mini-course bundle**, offering a clear solution for businesses needing fast growth. The result? Within two months, my first ₹50,000 project came from a referral.

Exercise:
Write down **3 core problems** you solve. Next, define **how your network can benefit** if they collaborate with or hire you.

Step 2: Package Offers for Different Segments

Not everyone in your network has the same needs or budget. Structuring **tiered offerings** can help you monetize efficiently:

1. **Low-ticket offers:** Short workshops, eBooks, or mini-services.
2. **Mid-ticket offers:** Monthly subscriptions, consulting sessions, or bundled services.
3. **High-ticket offers:** Premium coaching, joint ventures, or long-term retainers.

Personal Tip:
I started with small, affordable consulting sessions for beginners in my field. Those who got results upgraded to higher-tier packages. This tiered approach allowed me to monetize without overwhelming my audience.

Exercise:
Create **1 low-ticket, 1 mid-ticket, and 1 high-ticket offer** based on your skills and network.

Step 3: Leverage Collaborations for Revenue

Your network isn't just for advice—it can **actively generate income** through collaborations:

- **Joint offers:** Partner with a peer to sell a combined product or service.
- **Affiliate collaborations:** Promote others' services for a commission.
- **Referral programs:** Incentivize network connections to refer clients.

I partnered with a content creator to offer a "Brand + Marketing Bundle." Our audiences overlapped but were not identical. The bundle sold out in the first week, generating revenue neither of us could have achieved alone.

Exercise:

Identify **1 potential partner** in your network and draft a **collaboration proposal** that benefits both parties financially.

Step 4: Build a Monetization Funnel

Turning attention into income requires a **simple system**:

1. **Attract:** Share valuable content consistently.
2. **Engage:** Build trust through interactions, comments, and personal messages.
3. **Offer:** Present products or services that solve specific problems.
4. **Deliver:** Provide excellent results to encourage referrals and repeat business.

Personal Tip:

I created a mini funnel using my network: social media posts → free consultation → paid mini-course. Even without paid ads, my first ₹1,00,000 came purely from my connections and network trust.

Exercise:

Sketch a **3-step funnel** for monetizing your personal brand using your network: attract → engage → offer.

Step 5: Continuous Value Creation

Monetization isn't a one-time act; it's an ongoing process:

- Keep educating and inspiring your network.
- Provide results first; selling comes naturally afterward.
- Collect feedback to improve your offers.

After delivering a successful consulting project, I stayed in touch with clients, shared updates, and offered advanced solutions. Many returned for higher-ticket services, and several referred me to their network. Continuous value turned initial income into recurring revenue.

Exercise:

Create a **3-month content & engagement plan** for your network. Include tips, advice, and small offers that maintain trust while opening monetization opportunities.

Key Takeaways

- Monetization starts with clarity on your **unique value**.
- Tiered offerings help serve multiple audience segments effectively.
- Collaborations multiply revenue without multiplying effort.
- A simple funnel converts attention into consistent income.
- Continuous value creation ensures long-term monetization and trust.

Remember: **Your brand and network are your most powerful assets. Monetize ethically, provide real value, and your income will naturally follow.**

Next Exercises:

1. Define 3 problems you solve and how your network benefits.
2. Create a low, mid, and high-ticket offer.
3. Draft 1 collaboration proposal.
4. Sketch a monetization funnel for your personal brand.
5. Plan a 3-month engagement strategy to provide value and maintain monetization.

18

Automating Your Hustle

"Work smarter, not harder, and let your systems do the heavy lifting."

Have you ever felt like you're spinning your wheels, working endless hours on your side hustle but never seeing the freedom or growth you imagined? What if I told you that the same hustle could earn more **while you sleep**, simply by setting up the right systems?

When I started juggling multiple side hustles, I realized that **time is finite, but money can scale infinitely**—if you automate smartly. At first, I tried doing everything myself—emails, client onboarding, payments, follow-ups—and it was exhausting. That's when I discovered the true power of **automation**.

Step 1: Identify Repetitive Tasks

Automation starts by spotting tasks that **repeat daily or weekly**:

- Responding to emails or inquiries
- Client onboarding and follow-up
- Social media posting
- Payment collection
- Delivering digital products

In my first freelance venture, I spent 10–15 hours a week sending emails and scheduling calls. Once I automated follow-ups and appointment bookings, I freed 8 hours weekly—hours I reinvested in creating new offerings. That alone increased my revenue by 20% in the first month.

Exercise:

List 5 tasks in your side hustle that **repeat weekly or monthly**. Highlight the ones that **consume the most time**.

Step 2: Choose Simple Tools

You don't need complex systems to start automating:

- **Email Automation:** MailerLite, ConvertKit, or Gmail auto-responders
- **Scheduling Tools:** Calendly or Google Calendar
- **Payment & Delivery:** Razorpay, PayPal, or Gumroad
- **Social Media Scheduling:** Buffer, Hootsuite, or Canva Scheduler

Personal Tip:

I started with MailerLite for email sequences and Calendly for appointments. I didn't buy expensive software; I started with **tools that were free or low-cost**, then scaled as my revenue grew.

Exercise:

Pick **2 automation tools** you can implement this month. Write down **what task each tool will automate**.

Step 3: Create Standardized Processes

Automation isn't just tools; it's **processes that can run themselves**:

1. Define your workflow step-by-step.
2. Identify where technology or templates can replace manual effort.

3. Test and refine until the system works reliably.

For one of my digital courses, I created a **standard onboarding workflow**: purchase → automated welcome email → access to course → follow-up email for feedback. Once set, it ran smoothly without me lifting a finger, while students felt personally guided.

Exercise:
Write a **step-by-step process for one part of your hustle** (e.g., client onboarding, delivering a service, or content distribution) and mark steps you can automate.

Step 4: Automate Marketing & Sales

Your hustle doesn't grow if you rely solely on manual outreach. Automation in marketing is a game-changer:

- **Email Sequences:** Nurture leads automatically over time
- **Social Media Automation:** Schedule posts, stories, or tweets in advance
- **Sales Funnels:** Pre-designed funnels can convert leads into paying clients while you focus on creating new offers

I once launched a mini-course using a pre-built funnel. Leads signed up, got automated emails, and purchased without me interacting directly. The first launch earned ₹80,000 while I spent that week working on a new project.

Exercise:
Draft a **mini marketing funnel** you can automate within the next 30 days. Include lead capture, automated emails, and a simple offer.

Step 5: Delegate & Outsource

Automation is not just tech—it's also **leveraging people**:

- Hire virtual assistants for repetitive tasks
- Use freelancers for content creation or editing
- Delegate customer support with scripts or chatbots

When my freelance workload doubled, I hired a VA for customer queries. By training them on scripts and templates, they handled 80% of tasks I used to do. That freed my time to develop high-ticket offers, tripling my revenue in six months.

Exercise:

List **1 task you can outsource this month**, write a clear instruction sheet, and research a freelancer or VA platform.

Step 6: Measure & Optimize

Automation isn't "set and forget." You need **tracking and tweaking**:

- Monitor key metrics: sales, leads, and engagement
- Track time saved and tasks completed automatically
- Adjust sequences, workflows, and offers to improve conversions

I automated my email campaigns, but after 2 months, open rates dropped. I analyzed the sequence, tweaked subject lines and messaging, and saw engagement spike by 30%. Systems work best when continuously refined.

Exercise:

Choose **1 automated process** and define **3 KPIs to track success** this month.

Key Takeaways

- Identify repetitive tasks and automate them first.
- Start with simple, low-cost tools before scaling.
- Standardized processes make your hustle scalable.
- Automation can handle marketing, sales, and delivery.
- Delegate repetitive tasks to free your time.
- Track, analyze, and refine constantly.

Remember: **Automation doesn't remove the need for effort—it multiplies it. Set up smart systems, and watch your hustle grow while you focus on what matters most.**

Next Exercises:

1. List 5 repetitive tasks and choose 2 to automate immediately.
2. Select 2 tools to implement this month.
3. Create a step-by-step process for one core task and mark automation points.
4. Draft a mini automated marketing funnel.
5. Identify 1 task to outsource and create clear instructions.
6. Define 3 KPIs for one automated process to track improvements.

19

Scaling & Leveraging Your Hustle Network

"*Your network is your net worth.*" – Porter Gale

Have you ever wondered why some side hustlers seem to explode overnight while others struggle to gain traction despite working equally hard? The secret often isn't more hours—it's **who you know, how you connect, and how you leverage your network**.

When I first started my side hustles, I thought I had to do everything myself. I hustled, created, marketed, and sold alone. Months passed, and growth felt slow. Then I realized: **the right connections could accelerate everything**—more clients, more referrals, and even collaborative opportunities I hadn't imagined.

Step 1: Map Your Current Network

Begin by understanding your starting point. Your current network includes:

- Friends and family
- Colleagues and former classmates

- Social media connections
- Communities, forums, or clubs you participate in

I once reached out to a college friend I hadn't spoken to in years. A simple "Hey, I'm building a digital course, do you know anyone who might benefit?" turned into my **first 5 paying clients**. That moment taught me: **you don't need a huge network; you need the right outreach.**

Exercise:

Write down 10 people in your current network who could help you grow your side hustle. Include their contact info and how you might reach out.

Step 2: Expand Strategically

Your goal is **quality over quantity**. Focus on connections that:

- Align with your niche
- Complement your skills
- Could provide mentorship or collaboration opportunities

I joined a small online community of freelance coaches. By engaging consistently, sharing value, and helping others, I landed **3 collaborations** that generated ₹50,000 in extra revenue over two months.

Exercise:

Identify 3 online or offline communities that align with your hustle. Plan to **engage actively for at least 30 minutes a day** for the next week.

Step 3: Build Mutually Beneficial Relationships

Networking isn't asking for favors; it's about creating **win-win situations**. Think:

- What value can you provide before asking for anything?
- How can collaboration help both parties grow?

I offered to guest post for another freelancer's blog in exchange for exposure to their audience. That single post brought **over 200 potential leads** and 2 new clients. By giving first, I received much more than I expected.

Exercise:

List 3 ways you can **add value to someone in your network** this month without asking for anything in return.

Step 4: Leverage Referrals & Testimonials

Referrals are **one of the fastest ways to scale**:

- Ask happy clients for introductions
- Encourage reviews and testimonials
- Offer referral incentives when appropriate

After completing a project for one client, I casually asked, "Do you know anyone else who might benefit?" That single referral turned into **a recurring project worth ₹30,000/month**. Testimonials on my social media also attracted inquiries without me chasing clients.

Exercise:

Draft a **referral request script** or testimonial request template you can send to your next 5 satisfied clients.

Step 5: Collaborate Strategically

Collaborations multiply reach and credibility:

- Co-create content with peers

- Launch joint offers
- Partner for webinars or workshops

I co-hosted a webinar with a content creator in a complementary niche. Our combined audience **doubled registration**, and I gained **10 high-ticket clients** in one week. Collaboration didn't just increase revenue; it increased my **credibility and authority**.

Exercise:

List 2 potential collaborators in your niche. Plan **one joint project** you could execute in the next 60 days.

Step 6: Track & Scale Your Network

Just like your side hustle, your network requires strategy:

- Track outreach: messages sent, follow-ups, collaborations initiated
- Review results: new clients, opportunities, partnerships
- Double down on high-impact relationships

I kept a simple Google Sheet tracking every outreach effort. After three months, I realized **20% of my contacts were producing 80% of results**. I focused on nurturing these high-value relationships and scaled my business faster than ever.

Exercise:

Create a simple **network tracking sheet**. Include name, contact, relationship type, last interaction, and potential opportunities. Review weekly.

Key Takeaways

- Map your existing network and understand its potential.
- Expand strategically with quality connections.
- Provide value first; networking is a two-way street.
- Leverage referrals, testimonials, and collaborations.
- Track and focus on high-impact relationships.

Remember: **Your network is a living ecosystem. Nurture it, leverage it wisely, and it will multiply your income, opportunities, and freedom.**

Next Exercises:

1. List 10 people in your current network and plan outreach.
2. Identify 3 communities to engage with for growth.
3. List 3 ways to add value to someone this month.
4. Draft referral/testimonial request templates.
5. Identify 2 potential collaborators and plan a joint project.
6. Track outreach and results using a simple sheet.

20

Monetizing Your Brand & Network

"You don't get paid for what you know, you get paid for what you share." – Robin Sharma

Have you ever felt that building a brand and networking is exciting—but you're not quite sure **how to turn it into real income**? Many side hustlers invest hours in content creation, community engagement, and collaboration, yet revenue doesn't follow.

The secret lies in **strategically monetizing your brand and network** without feeling pushy or salesy.

When I started, I struggled with this. I had a small, engaged following online, clients loved my work, and opportunities came knocking—but I didn't know **how to convert attention into sustainable income**.

Over time, I discovered the power of structured monetization, and it transformed my side hustles into real, recurring revenue streams.

Step 1: Identify Your Monetization Paths

Every brand has multiple ways to monetize:

- **Products:** digital courses, eBooks, guides
- **Services:** coaching, consulting, freelancing
- **Affiliate partnerships:** promoting products you believe in
- **Events & workshops:** webinars, paid live sessions
- **Sponsored content:** collaborations with brands

I began monetizing my brand with **freelancing and small workshops**. Soon, I added an eBook and online course, creating **three simultaneous income streams**. By diversifying, I avoided dependency on a single revenue source and increased total income by 5x in 6 months.

Exercise:
List **all possible ways you could monetize your brand or network**. Highlight at least 2 that you can implement within the next 30 days.

Step 2: Packaging Your Offer

The way you **present your product or service** determines its value perception:

- Bundle small wins into higher-value packages
- Offer tiered pricing for beginners → intermediate → advanced users
- Add bonuses to increase perceived value

I created a **3-tier online course package**: Basic (self-study), Premium (with live Q&A), and Elite (personal coaching). This simple structure allowed clients to choose their comfort level while maximizing my revenue from the same audience.

Exercise:

Take your product/service idea and **draft a 3-tier offer** with clear benefits for each level.

Step 3: Leveraging Your Network

Your connections are one of the fastest paths to monetization:

- Offer your services to peers and collaborators
- Request referrals from trusted contacts
- Partner for joint offers to access new audiences

A peer I collaborated with introduced me to their audience via a **joint webinar**. Within one week, I signed **5 new clients**, earning more than my usual month's revenue from a single session. Networking is not just about visibility—it's about creating **mutually beneficial opportunities that convert into income.**

Exercise:

Identify **3 key people in your network** you can collaborate with to monetize your brand this month. Outline the type of collaboration and expected results.

Step 4: Content as a Revenue Engine

Your brand content can directly lead to income:

- Use blogs, social media, or newsletters to educate and build authority
- Embed subtle calls-to-action (CTAs) for products/services
- Repurpose content across platforms to increase reach

I wrote a **10-part content series on side hustles** and embedded links to my mini-course. This campaign alone generated **₹50,000 in sales in 2 weeks** without spending a single rupee on ads. Authority plus strategic CTAs equals monetization.

Exercise:

Plan **one content series** that positions you as an expert and promotes your offer. Include at least **2 subtle CTAs** within it.

Step 5: Creating Recurring Revenue Streams

Recurring income is the key to financial freedom:

- Subscription-based services (membership communities, coaching programs)
- Retainers for ongoing services
- Digital products with automated delivery

I launched a **membership program for freelancers**, providing weekly workshops and templates. Within 3 months, it became my **largest and most predictable income stream**, giving me confidence to scale my other side hustles.

Exercise:

Brainstorm **one recurring income idea** you can implement in the next 60 days. Outline the structure, pricing, and delivery method.

Step 6: Tracking and Optimizing

To grow your monetization strategy:

- Track conversions from your network and content
- Monitor which monetization paths produce the highest ROI
- Double down on the most profitable strategies

By tracking which posts and collaborations generated the most clients, I focused my efforts on high-converting opportunities. Within 6 months, my revenue **tripled**, and I spent less time chasing low-return efforts.

Exercise:

Set up a **simple tracking sheet**: columns for monetization method, outreach, conversions, and revenue. Review weekly and adjust your strategy.

Key Takeaways

- Diversify your monetization paths to reduce risk
- Package offers to maximize perceived value
- Leverage your network strategically for new clients and collaborations
- Use content to educate, build authority, and convert
- Focus on creating recurring revenue streams for predictable income
- Track and optimize every monetization effort

Remember: **Your network and brand are not just for visibility—they are your business engine. Monetize wisely, and your side hustles can transform into sustainable wealth.**

Next Exercises:

1. List all possible ways to monetize your brand or network.
2. Draft a 3-tier offer for your primary product/service.
3. Identify 3 collaborators in your network and plan a monetization activity.
4. Create a content series with embedded CTAs for your offer.
5. Brainstorm a recurring income stream with delivery method and pricing.
6. Track conversions and optimize for maximum ROI.

21

Automating Your Hustle

"Work smarter, not harder." – Allen F. Morgenstern

Have you ever wondered why some side hustlers seem to **earn more while working less**, while you feel stuck trading hours for money? The secret is **automation**. When you automate repetitive tasks, your hustle grows **without burning you out**, freeing time for strategy, creativity, and scaling.

When I first started, I spent **6–8 hours a day manually managing clients, invoices, and emails.** I was exhausted but not growing. It wasn't until I discovered the power of automation—tools, workflows, and templates—that I could **multiply my results** without multiplying my work hours.

Step 1: Identify Repetitive Tasks

The first step in automation is **spotting what drains your time**:

- Client onboarding
- Scheduling appointments
- Social media posting
- Email follow-ups

- Invoice creation

I realized that **sending individual emails to clients and reminding them for payments** consumed almost 2 hours daily. Automating this with templates and reminders instantly freed up 10+ hours per week, which I invested in **creating new offers**.

Exercise:
List **all recurring tasks in your hustle** that consume more than 30 minutes daily. Highlight the **top 3 you can automate immediately**.

Step 2: Leverage Automation Tools

There are countless **tools designed to automate your hustle**:

- **Email automation:** MailerLite, ConvertKit, or ActiveCampaign
- **Social media scheduling:** Buffer, Later, or Hootsuite
- **Project management:** Trello, Notion, or Asana
- **Invoices & payments:** QuickBooks, PayPal, or Razorpay
- **Task automation:** Zapier, Make, or IFTTT

I integrated **Zapier with my email and CRM**, so whenever a new client signed up, they received a welcome email, invoice, and onboarding link automatically. This eliminated repetitive admin work and reduced errors.

Exercise:
Pick **2 tools** you will implement this week to automate tasks in your hustle. Write down **specific tasks each tool will handle**.

Step 3: Create Repeatable Workflows

Automation isn't just tools—it's also **structured processes**:

- Map out your workflow from lead to payment
- Identify which steps are manual
- Automate wherever possible

I created a **lead-to-client workflow**: lead capture → automated email series → consultation call → invoice → follow-up → welcome email. This system **runs on autopilot**, allowing me to handle more clients without extra effort.

Exercise:
Sketch your **main hustle workflow** in words (step-by-step). Identify at least **2 steps that can be automated.**

Step 4: Automate Content & Marketing

Content is king, but it can also be time-consuming:

- Schedule social media posts in advance
- Use email sequences to nurture leads
- Repurpose content across platforms
- Track performance automatically

I used a **content calendar and scheduling tool** to post on LinkedIn, YouTube, and Instagram without logging in daily. My email newsletter nurtured leads automatically, resulting in **5–10 new clients every month** with almost zero manual effort.

Exercise:
Plan a **1-month content calendar** and identify which parts can be **fully automated**.

Step 5: Automate Client Communication

Communication is critical, but it can consume hours:

- Use **templates for FAQs** and common queries
- Automate follow-ups for payments, deadlines, and reminders
- Set up **chatbots** for basic customer queries

I implemented a **WhatsApp automation system** for client reminders. No more chasing payments or sending repetitive instructions. Clients loved the efficiency, and I gained more time to **focus on high-value work**.

Exercise:
Identify **3 communication tasks you perform daily**. Write down **how you can automate each task** using email, chat, or messaging tools.

Step 6: Test, Optimize, and Scale

Automation is not set-and-forget:

- Test your systems regularly
- Look for bottlenecks
- Scale what works while adjusting what doesn't

After automating my workflow, I noticed a few clients weren't receiving emails correctly. Adjusting triggers and sequences took a few hours but saved **hundreds of manual hours** in the long run. Optimization is the **secret multiplier**.

Exercise:
Set a **weekly review routine** to check your automated systems. Note 1 thing to **improve or optimize** each week.

Key Takeaways

- Identify repetitive tasks that drain your time
- Leverage tools to automate emails, content, payments, and client workflows
- Create repeatable processes that run independently
- Automate marketing, communication, and content to scale faster
- Test, optimize, and refine automation systems for maximum efficiency

Remember: **Automation is the engine that allows your side hustles to grow while you focus on strategic actions, creativity, and scaling to multiple income streams.**

Next Exercises:

1. List all repetitive tasks in your hustle and identify top 3 for immediate automation.
2. Choose 2 automation tools and map the tasks they will handle.
3. Write out your main workflow in words and mark automation opportunities.
4. Plan a 1-month content calendar and automation schedule.
5. Identify 3 communication tasks to automate.
6. Set a weekly review routine to optimize automated systems.

22

Scaling Your Network & Collaborations

"*Your network is your net worth.*" – Porter Gale

Have you ever noticed how some side hustlers seem to **always find the right opportunities, clients, or partners** while others struggle alone? The secret isn't just luck—it's **strategic networking and collaborations**. The right connections **multiply your growth**, open doors to new markets, and create income streams you never imagined.

When I first started my side hustles, I tried doing everything alone. I was grinding 12 hours a day, yet my growth was slow. Everything changed when I **actively built a network of mentors, peers, and collaborators**. Suddenly, opportunities started flowing in, joint projects increased my credibility, and I could focus on high-value tasks instead of reinventing the wheel.

Step 1: Identify Your Key Network Groups

Before you can scale your network, you need to **know who matters most**:

- **Mentors:** Experienced individuals who can guide you
- **Peers:** People hustling in the same or complementary niches
- **Clients/Customers:** Your future advocates and repeat clients

- **Collaborators:** People you can create joint projects with

I started by making a list of **10 people I admired** in my industry. I reached out to them with genuine interest, asking questions, sharing insights, and offering value. Within 6 months, I had **3 mentors and multiple peer collaborations** that accelerated my growth far beyond what I could achieve alone.

Exercise:

Write down **5–10 people** you want in each category: mentor, peer, client, collaborator. Note one actionable way to **connect with each person this month.**

Step 2: Build Relationships, Not Transactions

Networking isn't about asking for favors immediately—it's about **providing value.**

- Share knowledge freely
- Support peers and collaborators
- Celebrate others' wins
- Be consistent in communication

I reached out to a fellow freelancer offering a free **review of their marketing funnel**. That small gesture led to a **long-term collaboration** and multiple client referrals. The key was building **trust before expecting anything in return**.

Exercise:

Identify **3 people in your network** you can provide value to this week. Write down **specific ways to help them** without expecting anything in return.

Step 3: Leverage Online Platforms

Your network doesn't have to be local. Online platforms make **connecting globally** easier than ever:

- LinkedIn: Build credibility, post insights, engage in discussions
- Instagram/YouTube: Showcase your expertise and collaborate with peers
- Forums & Communities: Engage in niche-specific groups

By consistently posting actionable tips on LinkedIn, I attracted **mentorship offers, collaboration proposals, and freelance leads** from people I had never met in person.

Exercise:

Pick **2 online platforms** where your audience or peers hang out. Commit to **posting or engaging 3 times per week** this month. Track connections made.

Step 4: Initiate Collaborations

Collaboration is a **force multiplier** for side hustles:

- Joint webinars or workshops
- Co-created content or courses
- Affiliate partnerships
- Shared projects or consulting

I collaborated with a content creator who had a complementary skill set. We launched a mini-course together. The **revenue split was small**, but the **brand exposure and new clients** I gained were priceless.

Exercise:

Identify **2 potential collaborators** this month. Outline a **small project** you can do together within 30 days.

Step 5: Maintain & Nurture Your Network

Building your network is just the beginning; you need to **maintain relationships**:

- Send updates on wins, projects, or milestones
- Offer help before asking for it
- Schedule periodic check-ins
- Celebrate others' successes publicly

I make it a habit to **message 5 key contacts every week**, sharing a helpful tip or congratulating them on achievements. This simple practice keeps my network active, engaged, and ready for future collaborations.

Exercise:
Create a **weekly networking habit**. List 5 contacts you will engage with and what value you will provide.

Step 6: Track Your Growth

Just like income and side hustles, your network **requires tracking and strategy**:

- Track collaborations and their outcomes
- Monitor new leads or opportunities from your network
- Evaluate what types of connections provide the **highest growth potential**

I maintained a simple document tracking **every collaboration, lead, and referral**. This helped me **double my side hustle revenue in 6 months** just by focusing on the right relationships.

Exercise:

Start a **Network Tracker** in a notebook or spreadsheet. Record each new connection, engagement, and outcome. Review monthly for opportunities to improve.

Key Takeaways

- Focus on mentors, peers, clients, and collaborators
- Build relationships by **providing value first**
- Leverage online platforms to scale your reach
- Initiate small, mutually beneficial collaborations
- Maintain, nurture, and track your network regularly
- Treat your network as a **growth engine**, not just contacts

Remember: **A strong network multiplied with automation and scalable side hustles is the formula for building financial freedom faster than going it alone.**

Next Exercises:

1. List 5–10 key people in each network category: mentors, peers, clients, collaborators.
2. Offer value to 3 people this week without expecting anything in return.
3. Commit to 2 online platforms for engagement and posting.
4. Identify 2 potential collaborations and outline a mini-project.
5. Set up a weekly habit to nurture your top 5 connections.
6. Start a network tracker to measure growth and outcomes.

23

Monetizing Your Brand & Network

"Your network isn't just for connections—it's a goldmine waiting to be activated."

Have you ever wondered why some side hustlers seem to **effortlessly turn contacts into clients, collaborations into revenue, and influence into income**? The secret isn't just working hard—it's **strategically monetizing your brand and network**.

When I first realized the power of my network, I had hundreds of connections but **no system to leverage them**. One small change—**treating relationships as opportunities to provide value while creating mutual benefit**—transformed my side hustles into sustainable income streams.

Suddenly, my collaborations were generating consistent revenue, and my personal brand attracted new clients without cold outreach.

Step 1: Identify Monetizable Relationships

Not every connection will generate revenue, but **some relationships can unlock high-value opportunities**:

- Collaborators for joint projects
- Mentors who can introduce you to high-ticket clients
- Peers who can exchange leads
- Audience members or followers ready to invest

I had a mentor who connected me to a client willing to pay **₹50,000 for a consulting session**. That single introduction more than doubled my side hustle revenue that month.

Exercise:

List **5 people in your network** who could become clients, collaborators, or referral partners. Note **one actionable step to approach each** this month.

Step 2: Offer High-Value Solutions

Monetization requires **packaging your expertise** in a way people are willing to pay for:

- Small digital products (templates, guides, mini-courses)
- Services (freelancing, consulting, coaching)
- Joint ventures (webinars, co-branded products)

I created a **mini-course priced at ₹999** for beginners in my niche. By leveraging my existing network and past collaborators for promotion, I sold **over 200 copies in the first month**.

Exercise:

Identify **one high-value product or service** you can offer this month to your network. Write down **3 ways to market it** through existing connections.

Step 3: Turn Followers into Customers

Your personal brand and content create trust. Monetization happens when you **guide your audience from free value to paid solutions**:

- Share helpful tips, stories, and case studies
- Introduce your paid services naturally
- Highlight results and testimonials from early clients

I shared a personal story on LinkedIn about **how I scaled a side hustle to ₹10,000/month**. The post received engagement, and several connections signed up for my consulting services—without me sending a single direct sales message.

Exercise:

Draft **one story-driven post** showcasing a small win or result. Include a subtle call-to-action for your product or service.

Step 4: Collaborations as Revenue Streams

Monetizing your network isn't just about selling; it's about **creating mutually beneficial partnerships**:

- Co-create a product with a peer
- Launch a joint webinar with a collaborator
- Exchange services or cross-promote

I collaborated with another freelancer to host a **webinar on building digital side hustles**. Our combined audiences paid ₹499 each, and we split the revenue while gaining **long-term email subscribers and repeat clients**.

Exercise:

Identify **2 collaborators** and brainstorm a small project or offer you can launch together within 30 days.

Step 5: Track and Optimize Revenue

Just like a side hustle, monetizing your network **requires measurement and optimization**:

- Track which collaborations generate the highest revenue
- Measure engagement vs. conversion
- Refine offers and messaging for maximum impact

By tracking the **source of each client and collaboration**, I realized that LinkedIn connections and past collaborators generated **3x more revenue than cold outreach**. I shifted focus accordingly, doubling my income in 90 days.

Exercise:

Create a **Revenue Tracker**: List all income sources from your network, note the type (collaboration, client, affiliate, product), and measure revenue monthly.

Key Takeaways

- Focus on **high-value relationships** that can generate revenue
- Offer solutions your network is willing to pay for
- Use your personal brand to **convert followers into customers**
- Collaborate strategically for mutual benefit and increased reach
- Track results and optimize continuously

Remember: **Your network, when properly leveraged, can become a consistent and scalable revenue engine—turning side hustles into sustainable wealth and financial freedom.**

Next Exercises:

1. List 5 connections in your network to monetize this month.
2. Identify one high-value service, product, or offer to market.
3. Draft a story-driven post guiding followers toward your offer.
4. Plan 2 collaboration projects with peers or mentors.
5. Set up a monthly revenue tracker to monitor network monetization.

24

Automating Your Hustle

"Work smarter, not harder. Systems turn effort into consistent results."

Have you ever felt like no matter how much you hustle, **there aren't enough hours in the day** to grow your side business? The truth is, **manual effort alone caps your income and freedom.** Automation allows you to **scale your side hustles while freeing up time,** so you can focus on growth, creativity, and high-value tasks.

When I first started, I spent hours manually sending emails, posting content, and managing clients. It was exhausting. Once I implemented simple systems—**automated email follow-ups, scheduling tools, and workflow templates**—my productivity skyrocketed, and my revenue started growing even when I wasn't actively working.

Step 1: Identify Repetitive Tasks

Automation begins with **spotting tasks that repeat daily or weekly**:

- Email follow-ups
- Social media posting
- Client onboarding

- Content repurposing

I realized I was **spending 3–4 hours per week manually sending follow-ups** to potential clients. Once I set up an automated email sequence, the same clients were contacted automatically, saving me 12–16 hours per month—time I used to create new products and grow my network.

Exercise:

Make a list of **all repetitive tasks in your side hustle**. Highlight **3 tasks you could automate this month**.

Step 2: Choose Simple Tools

Automation doesn't have to be complex or expensive. For beginners:

- **Email Automation:** MailerLite, ConvertKit, or free Gmail templates
- **Social Media Scheduling:** Buffer, Canva Scheduler, or Later
- **Project & Workflow Management:** Trello, Notion, Asana
- **Payment & Invoicing:** PayPal, Stripe, Razorpay

I started with **free versions of MailerLite and Trello**. Even with minimal investment, I **saved 8–10 hours per week** and avoided missed follow-ups that could have cost me clients.

Exercise:

Pick **2 tools from the list above** and implement them this week. Track the time saved.

Step 3: Automate Client Onboarding

Every client or customer experience should be **smooth, consistent, and mostly automated**:

- Create a **welcome email sequence**
- Share instructions, deliverables, and payment links automatically
- Include FAQs and support resources

I created an **automated onboarding email sequence** for my consulting clients. Instead of spending an hour per client explaining processes, clients now receive all details automatically. This allowed me to **handle more clients without extra effort**.

Exercise:
Draft a **3-step onboarding email sequence** for your clients or customers this month.

Step 4: Repurpose & Automate Content

Content fuels your brand and network, but creating everything manually is unsustainable:

- Repurpose blog posts into videos, social media snippets, and email newsletters
- Use scheduling tools to **publish consistently without daily effort**

I took one LinkedIn article, turned it into **5 short posts, 1 video, and an email newsletter**, and scheduled them for the month. The same content generated **leads and engagement** while I focused on other revenue-generating tasks.

Exercise:

Choose **one piece of content** this week and plan **3 ways to repurpose it**. Schedule it using a tool.

Step 5: Automate Follow-Ups & Sales Funnels

Your network and audience can be monetized more efficiently with **simple sales funnels and follow-up systems**:

- Free lead magnet → Email sequence → Paid offer
- Reminder emails for abandoned carts or unclaimed offers
- Upsell or cross-sell follow-ups

I set up a **simple lead magnet funnel** for my side hustle. Leads who opted in automatically received **3 value-packed emails** before being presented with my paid course. Within a month, it generated **₹30,000+ in sales** without me manually messaging anyone.

Exercise:

Draft a **mini funnel for one of your products or services**: Lead magnet → 3 emails → paid offer.

Key Takeaways

- Identify repetitive tasks and focus on automating them first
- Use simple, beginner-friendly tools to save time
- Automate client onboarding, follow-ups, and content distribution
- Repurpose content to maximize reach without extra effort
- Use sales funnels to convert leads and network into consistent revenue

Remember: **Automation doesn't replace your creativity—it multiplies it. By systematizing repetitive work, you free your time to grow, innovate, and scale your side hustles toward real financial freedom.**

Next Exercises:

1. List 3 tasks to automate this month.
2. Pick 2 tools and implement automation.
3. Create a 3-step client onboarding sequence.
4. Repurpose one content piece into 3 formats.
5. Draft a mini funnel for a product or service.

25

Your Personal Action Plan & Next Steps

"A goal without a plan is just a wish." – Antoine de Saint-Exupéry

You've learned mindset shifts, side hustle strategies, brand-building, automation, and network growth. But all of this knowledge **only becomes powerful when you take action**. Are you ready to **turn your learning into results** and finally break free from the middle-class trap?

When I first started my journey, I felt overwhelmed. There were so many ideas, tools, and strategies that I didn't know where to begin. The solution was simple: **create a step-by-step action plan with small, measurable milestones**.

Today, that same approach has helped me scale multiple income streams, automate workflows, and build sustainable financial freedom.

Step 1: Set Your 6-Month Goals

Your goals should be **specific, measurable, and realistic**, yet ambitious enough to push you out of your comfort zone.

- Revenue targets: e.g., first ₹10k, ₹50k, ₹1 lakh
- Skill development: e.g., mastering content creation, freelancing platforms, or sales
- Network growth: connect with 10 mentors or collaborators

Exercise:
Write down **3 key goals for the next 6 months**. Include revenue, skills, and network targets.

Step 2: Break Goals into Monthly Milestones

Small wins build confidence and momentum. Divide your 6-month goals into **actionable monthly steps**:

- Month 1: Identify side hustle, choose tools, create first offer
- Month 2: Launch first product/service, gather feedback
- Month 3: Build email list, automate 1 task
- Month 4: Scale content, network, and collaborations
- Month 5: Refine automation, upsell or cross-sell offers
- Month 6: Review, measure, and plan for next 6 months

Exercise:
Create a **monthly milestone table** in paragraph form: write each month's main focus and 2–3 tasks you will accomplish.

Step 3: Daily & Weekly Action Steps

Consistency is key. Create **daily and weekly routines** that align with your milestones:

- Daily: 1 hour on skill development, 1 hour on side hustle

- Weekly: 1 networking session, 1 content piece, 1 automated task implemented

Exercise:

Write a **weekly action checklist**: what you will do every week for the next month to achieve your milestones.

Step 4: Build Accountability

Even the best plan can fail without accountability. Options include:

- Sharing your goals with a friend or mentor
- Joining a community or mastermind
- Tracking progress publicly in a journal or social media (optional)

When I started, I **shared my 30-day goals with a mentor**. This simple act kept me consistent and motivated, and I **achieved revenue targets faster than I imagined**.

Exercise:

Choose **one accountability method** and set it up this week.

Step 5: Review, Reflect, and Reinvest

Every month, **review your progress**:

- What worked?
- What didn't work?
- Which tasks can be automated or delegated?
- How can you reinvest earnings into your growth?

Exercise:

Write a **monthly reflection**: 3 things you learned, 2 things to improve, and 1 way to reinvest your earnings.

Step 6: Plan for Scaling

Once your first income streams are stable, think about **next-level growth**:

- Multiple side hustles
- Productized services
- Affiliate marketing and collaborations
- Automating further to free your time

After implementing small, consistent steps, I **scaled from earning ₹10k/-month to multiple revenue streams generating ₹1 lakh+ monthly**. Automation, smart networking, and reinvesting made it possible.

Exercise:

Write down **2 new ways to scale your side hustles** over the next 6 months.

Key Takeaways

- Action beats knowledge—implement step-by-step
- Break 6-month goals into monthly, weekly, and daily tasks
- Use accountability to stay consistent
- Reflect and reinvest consistently
- Always plan for scaling and automation

Remember: A side hustle isn't just a way to earn—it's your bridge to financial freedom. By following this action plan, you're taking control of your time, income, and future. Start small, stay consistent, and think big. Your freedom is waiting.

26

Invitations

Congratulations! You now have the roadmap to **shift your mindset and start building wealth**. If you're ready to **accelerate your journey**, I've created a complete online course that:

- Provides **step-by-step guidance** to start and scale your side hustle.
- Shares **templates, worksheets, and action plans** for beginners.
- Offers a **community of like-minded learners** for support and accountability.
- Includes **case studies and strategies** to fast-track your first ₹10k, ₹50k, and beyond.

Take the next step:

"Ready to take the next step? Explore my online courses, join live webinars, and access exclusive templates and blueprints to accelerate your journey from knowledge to real digital income. Visit www.takshaydigitalacademy.com *and start building your digital empire today!"*

Visit to join our courses

Join now and turn your side hustle into **real financial freedom**.

Series Companion Map – "Digital Wealth Ecosystem"

Here's how Book 12 fits into the **full 12-book ecosystem** and funnels you to courses and actionable income:

Step 1 – Mindset & Foundation

- Book 1: Digital Coach Blueprint
- Book 2: 10X Digital Coach Mastery
- Book 3: 10X Funnel Mindset Secrets

Step 2 – Ads, Funnels, and Business Skills

- Book 4: Meta Ads Secrets
- Book 5: Google Ads Secrets
- Book 6: Digital Empire

Step 3 – Financial Mindset & Side Hustle Growth

- Book 7: Rock Bottom to Digital Freedom
- Book 8: Middle-Class Trap to Millionaire Mindset
- Book 9: Side Hustle to Financial Freedom

Step 4 – AI & Social Media Mastery

- Book 10: Decode YouTube Algorithm
- Book 11: Decode Instagram Algorithm
- Book 12: The AI Millionaire

Step 5 – Courses & Live Coaching

- Use these books as your **roadmap to digital freedom**
- Each book includes exercises, worksheets, and companion resources

- Join courses and webinars to scale faster and automate income

27

Join our Community

Let's Stay Connected

AUTHOR :- TARUN TAKSHAY

The author would like to interact with you and receive your feedback. Get in touch and send him your reviews

www.takshaydigitalacademy.com
www.taruntakshay.com
tarun@taruntakshay.com
www.youtube.com/digitaltakshay
www.instagram.com/taruntakshay
www.facebook.com/taruntakshay
https://www.linkedin.com/in/tarun-takshay/
https://digitaltakshay.com/

To know more check out www.taruntakshay.com

Thank you !

This book may end here, but our journey together doesn't have to. I'd love to hear your story—what resonated with you, what breakthroughs you experienced, and how you're applying these systems in your coaching business.

📧 You can reach me directly at: **info@takshaydigitalacademy.com**

🌐 Or visit my website: https://www.takshaydigitalacademy.com/

You can also connect with me on social media to get updates, free resources, and ongoing mentorship. Just search for **"Tarun Takshay"** and join the community.

28

Conclusion

By now, you've learned:

- How to identify and launch your first side hustle
- Mindset shifts to overcome fear and procrastination
- Time management and productivity hacks for side hustle growth
- Branding, networking, and collaboration to amplify results
- Scaling, automation, and creating multiple streams of income

The next step is **action**. Knowledge alone doesn't change your life; consistent execution does. Use the **6-month action plan**, reflect, and scale. Keep learning, experimenting, and reinvesting in your growth.

Remember, financial freedom isn't a distant dream—it's a **series of small wins, compounded consistently**. You now have the tools, mindset, and roadmap. It's your turn to act.

Start today. Small consistent steps will transform your life.

Epilogue

"Don't live the same year 75 times and call it a life." – Robin Sharma

"The best way to predict your future is to create it." – Abraham Lincoln

"Small daily improvements over time lead to stunning results." – Robin Sharma

Afterword

I wrote this book because I've been where you are: unsure, frustrated, and dreaming of something bigger. Over the years, I've experimented, failed, and learned lessons the hard way. Through this book, I want to **share practical, actionable strategies** so you don't have to make the same mistakes I did.

Every chapter is crafted to **teach, motivate, and guide you step-by-step**. You'll find exercises, personal stories, and insights that are realistic for anyone balancing jobs, family, and life responsibilities.

I encourage you to **take notes, complete the exercises, and revisit your progress**. The knowledge you gain here is only valuable when applied.

www.ingramcontent.com/pod-product-compliance
Ingram Content Group UK Ltd.
Pitfield, Milton Keynes, MK11 3LW, UK
UKHW011513190726
13845UKWH00034B/1239

9 789356 357785